LOOKING AFTER

FRESHWATER

AQUARIUM

FISH

DAVID ALDERTON

BLANDFORD

First published in this edition in 1995 by Blandford
A Cassell imprint
Cassell plc
Wellington House
125 Strand
London WC2R 0BB

Distributed in the United States
by Sterling Publishing Co. Inc.
387 Park Lane South
New York, NY 10016–8810

Distributed in Australia by
Capricorn Link (Australia) Pty Ltd
2–13 Carrington Road, Castle Hill
NSW 2154

Printed and bound in Spain by Bookprint S.L.
Barcelona

British Library Cataloguing in Publication Data

Alderton, David
    Looking after aquarium fish
    1. Aquarium fish
    I. Title
    639.3′4   SF457

ISBN 0–7137–2580–X

Photographs by Hans Mayland

the information store

📞 01603 773114
email: tis@ccn.ac.uk

21 DAY LOAN ITEM

2 7 APR 2015

05

Please return <u>on or before</u> the last date stamped above

A fine will be charged for overdue items

 CITY COLLEGE NORWICH

Contents

Note
Figures in gallons are Imperial throughout
1 Imperial gallon = 4.55 litres
1 US gallon = 3.78 litres

PART I KEEPING FISH IN AQUARIA

Among the early cultures, the Egyptians kept fish in ponds, as did the Romans, although their interest was confined to providing a source of fresh food. It was in the East, however, that ornamental fish-keeping developed as a hobby. Goldfish (*Carassius auratus*) were known in China by the tenth century, although they did not reach Britain until 700 years later. They were often kept at monasteries and it is likely that ornamental strains were derived from the wild form of carp (*C. carassius*), which was again being kept for food. Other colour forms of the goldfish were soon being developed, and given exotic names such as 'Lotus Terrace' and 'Crane Pearl'. There was a particular pool near Peking, which became known as 'Goldfish Pond', and proved a popular spot where visitors could see and admire many of these new varieties.

There was considerable interest in goldfish in other countries of the Orient, notably Japan, which thus ensured that European travellers to the East soon encountered these 'little gilded fish', as one seventeenth-century writer described them. Within 100 years, they were breeding freely in Britain, and Horace Walpole was moved to write to his friend Montagu, requesting that he collected some goldfish soon, because Walpole himself was being overwhelmed with them.

Goldfish survive well in unheated surroundings, but by way of contrast, the guppy (*Poecilia reticulata*), which is now the most widely-kept tropical fish, was seen alive in Europe for the first time only as recently as 1908. This species occurs naturally in northern South America as well as some offshore islands, and in less than a century, it too has been thoroughly domesticated and is currently being bred in many forms.

A twentieth-century pastime

The development of tropical fish-keeping as a popular hobby has occurred almost exclusively during the twentieth century. Prior to this, the difficulties encountered in maintaining tanks were almost insurmountable, while the supply of fish was minimal. The reasons underlying the boom in tropical aquaria are closely linked to the rapid developments in technology which have taken place in the present century.

Air transport has enabled fish to be flown large distances in a relatively short space of time, and to arrive at their destinations in good health. In 1994, fish were imported from fifty countries around the world into Britain. The breeding and supply of fish has become a major international industry. The first fish farm in Florida was opened in 1926, and today, there are nearly 200 such enterprises here, directly employing 1000 people and generating 100 million dollars of revenue annually. Most freshwater aquarium fish are now bred on such farms, rather than being caught in the wild. One of the largest enterprises in Florida supplies eighteen million fish to the trade each year. This is far removed from the early years of the century when the few tropical fish which did reach Britain had to be sent from Europe by rail and sea, with over three-quarters of most consignments perishing *en route* during the two-day journey.

Today, when tropical fish arrive at their destinations, electrical apparatus can be used to maintain their environment at a constant temperature, and to help keep it clean and aerated. Since the 1960s, considerable strides have been made to facilitate the keeping of tropical fish in the home. Mass production of tanks and equipment, coupled with full utilization of new technology, has ensured that the cost of a tropical aquarium complete with fish is not prohibitive for the vast majority of people. In addition, the subsequent costs involved in maintaining and feeding the fish are minimal.

An aquarium also lends itself to a twentieth-century lifestyle. Unlike most other creatures, fish can be kept without difficulty in a very wide variety of domestic environments, in flats or apartments, for example, where other pets would be impractical. Their tanks will fit attractively in various locations, whether recessed into a wall or used as a room divider. Fish-keeping is also a very relaxing hobby, and it is no coincidence that in potentially stressful places, such as a dentist's waiting room, a tank of fish is often present.

There is considerable scope within the hobby for the enthusiast. Apart from keeping the wide array of both coldwater and tropical fish of all sizes and colours which are now available, fish breeding offers a fascinating and worthwhile pursuit. Aquarist societies exist in many regions, and often organize shows for their members. Such clubs provide an ideal opportunity to meet others with similar interests, and develop lasting friendships.

Adaptation

Fish occur in a wide range of aquatic environments, and observation of their shapes will often give an indication of their habits. Those which live close to the bottom, such as loaches or eels, generally resemble worms. Tall, thin fish, like angelfish, are found typically in reedy localities, where they hide and weave in and out

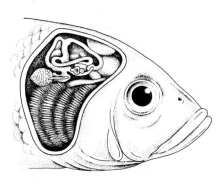

Head of Labyrinth fish cut away to illustrate the labyrinth organ, which enables these fish to breathe atmospheric air directly.

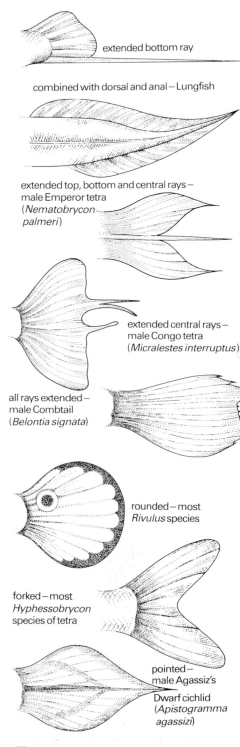

Left Angelfish (*Pterophyllum* species) occur in reedy areas.

extended bottom ray

combined with dorsal and anal – Lungfish

extended top, bottom and central rays – male Emperor tetra (*Nematobrycon palmeri*)

extended central rays – male Congo tetra (*Micralestes interruptus*)

all rays extended – male Combtail (*Belontia signata*)

rounded – most *Rivulus* species

forked – most *Hyphessobrycon* species of tetra

pointed – male Agassiz's Dwarf cichlid (*Apistogramma agassizi*)

Fin types.

of the vegetation. Fish found near the surface have a relatively straight back and a rounded belly, as seen in the case of the hatchetfish of South America, whereas fish occurring in the main body of water are more streamlined. The position of the mouth is also indicative of a fish's living habits. In loaches, it points downwards, whereas it sticks up in hatchetfish. The number and type of teeth present depends on the fish concerned, but serve to reveal its feeding habits. The sharp teeth of the piranha are legendary, even to those who have never kept fish.

In order to breath, fish rely largely on their gills to extract oxygen from the water. Other gases, such as carbon dioxide, are also excreted by this route. The gills themselves are located behind the eyes, with the rows of filaments protected by a cover on each side. Modifications of this pattern of respiration are seen in certain fish. The Labyrinth fish are able to breath atmospheric air directly through their gills, whereas others can utilize their swim-bladder, which is normally used for buoyancy, for respiratory purposes. Any interference with gill function is likely to have very serious effects on the fish itself.

The fish's sensory system differs significantly from that of a

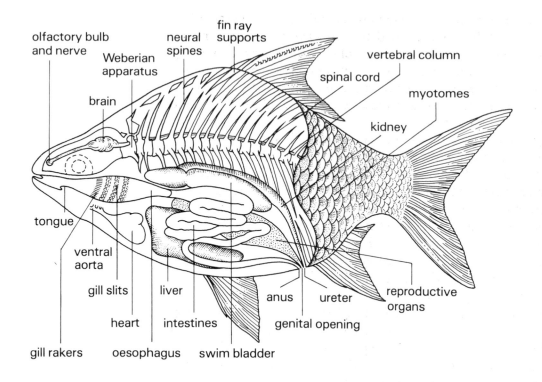

Internal anatomy of a fish.

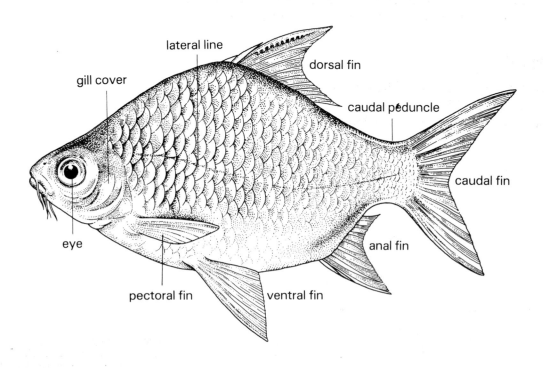

Anatomy of a fish.

mammal. The lateral line, which is visible along the length of the body in most fish, serves to detect changes in pressure in the external environment. The presence of both stationary and moving objects can be ascertained by this means. The pressure waves impinging on the fish's skin are then transmitted via the mucus in the canal to neuromasts, and these cells are linked directly to the brain by cerebral nerves.

Sight is a variable sense in fish, ranging from virtual lack of vision in the case of Blind Cave Fish to the highly developed visual acuity possessed by most fish which live near the water's surface. Whereas those found in clear waters usually have good sight, fish occurring in murky surroundings, such as various catfish, have a keen sense of smell. They also have barbels in the vicinity of their mouth which contain taste buds. Fish can prove quite adaptable, as shown in a Spiny Catfish (*Acanthordoras spinosissimus*) born without eyes, which immediately managed to feed itself by smell alone, and lived satisfactorily for years.

Under conditions of darkness, fish do not sleep in the same way as mammals, although they do become inactive and body processes are slowed. At dawn, they take approximately twenty minutes to become fully alert again, and often will not feed during this period.

Longevity of fish is an extremely variable characteristic. Certain Killifish may survive only a matter of months until their ponds dry up, but when kept in water constantly, some have lived for five years. Goldfish and catfish generally prove the longest-lived species under aquarium conditions, often living for a decade or more.

Healthy fish

Healthy fish move without difficulty, swimming evenly through the water. Those with ragged or frayed fins should be avoided if possible. Drooping fins are usually indicative of ill-thrift, although

Aphyosemion sjoestedti. These Killifish from West Africa live for a short time only, before the water in their pools evaporates.

in Fighting Fish, for example, this condition is quite normal. The eyes must not protrude unnaturally from their sockets, as this condition, known as pop-eye, is a sign of illness. The scales of the body should appear healthy, and be free from white spots and fungus. Larger parasites such as *Argulus* may be seen occasionally on the sides of fish, especially goldfish, and these can present problems. Most dealers go to great trouble to ensure their stock is healthy, but there are exceptions, and shops where dead fish are left floating in tanks alongside apparently healthy individuals should not be patronized. Although the remaining fish in the tank may appear healthy, the chances of them also succumbing to disease, following the stress of being moved, are significantly increased.

1 Tanks and Equipment

The traditional rectangular tank, constructed with an iron frame and putty to hold the glass in place, is now a rare sight in aquarist shops. The advent of silicone rubber sealant has led to a revolution in the design of tanks over the last two decades, enabling a much wider range of shapes to be created, freed from the constraints of an iron framework. Triangular tanks, for example, fitting neatly in the corner of a room are now quite often seen.

The sealer

Whereas putty eventually tends to dry out, causing the tank to leak, silicone rubber, having been applied to the glass surfaces and left to cure in air for forty-eight hours, forms a permanent bond. It does not set hard, but remains flexible and is thus able to absorb differing water pressures without its bonding power being compromized. With normal slight temperature changes causing both contraction and expansion in the tank glass, this is vital. When epoxy resin was tried instead as a tank sealer, leaks developed because the bonding in this case was too rigid.

Frameless tanks

As silicone rubber has a bonding power of 2068 kN per sq m (300 lb per sq in), the heavy iron framework of putty tanks is no longer required, and tanks are therefore lighter and cheaper as a result. Most people prefer to purchase a ready-made tank, but it is possible to make one to specific dimensions with relatively little difficulty. The actual size of the tank will be influenced in either case by the space available, and the fish which are to be kept in it. Adequate allowance must be made for their subsequent growth, so it is advisable to obtain a relatively large tank at the outset.

Tank sizes

The dimensions of the tank that give rise to the surface area of the water are vital, because this is where atmospheric oxygen diffuses into the water. If the length and width of the tank are too small, relative to its depth, then, with a large number of fish present, the water may contain insufficient oxygen to support them. While deeper tanks are necessary for large broad-bodied fish, like angelfish, as the depth increases it becomes progressively harder to light the lower levels effectively from above.

Although recommendations are made for the volume of water to be allowed per unit length of fish, these should not be considered as absolute figures, but interpreted as guidelines. Indeed, a tank that is stocked to its maximum limit at the outset will soon be over-crowded as its occupants increase in size.

Calculations

The calculations necessary to obtain the volume of a tank are quite simple, especially if metric dimensions are used. It is a matter of multiplying the length, width and depth measurements in centimetres together, and then finally dividing the total by 1000 to obtain the tank's capacity in litres. Ten per cent of this figure is then subtracted to allow for tank decoration, giving the functional capacity. For small fish, an allowance of 1½-2 litres per centimetre of length should be adequate, or approximately 1 gallon per inch using imperial units. A 30-litre tank will therefore support fish whose combined lengths do not exceed 15 cm (6 in). The figure for the true capacity of the tank will also be necessary if any treatments have to be added to the water, to ensure that the correct dilution is achieved.

Building tanks

Silicone rubber sealant is available in tubes with an attached nozzle dispenser for the prospective tank-builder. It is important to use aquarium sealant only, as other types may well contain chemicals that are toxic to fish. The saving in cost of building one's own tank against that of commercially-produced models is, however, usually marginal, unless an unusual design is required. The choice of glass for the tank is a vital consideration, both with regard to stability, and clarity of viewing. A minimum thickness of 6.4 mm (¼ in) should be used to form the tank's bottom, with 9.5 mm (⅜ in) preferable for 120 cm (48 in) tanks. As an additional safeguard for all tanks over 60 cm (24 in) in length, a suitable supporting beam positioned half-way along its length and running from front to back at the top is recommended. Alternatively, extra support can be given lengthways, with strips running from end to end of the two main panels. Located just below the top of the tank, these strips may also help to support the tank cover as well.

Float glass should be chosen for the front panel, but it is possible to economize by using rough cast glass for the remainder, although visibility will not be as good through these panels. Second-hand glass is not recommended, because it may contain minute imperfections, such as scratches, which weaken it.

Having decided on the dimensions, and with the pieces cut to size, the first stage is to smooth off the rough edges using fine-grade emery paper. The glass surfaces should be wetted at frequent intervals during this process, and finally washed off completely. When wet, the glass is particularly slippery, and needs to be handled with extra care. Once they have dried, the panels should be cleaned with a suitable solvent such as pure turpentine, to ensure that there are no remaining residues which could compromise the subsequent bonding of the silicone rubber with the glass. The final step before assembly is to wipe the surfaces over again thoroughly with clean paper tissue.

The actual construction of the tank is best carried out on a large table or clean workbench covered with newspaper to prevent accidental scratching of the glass. The base panel is first laid flat on top of the paper, and a thin line of sealant is drawn out along one edge. The glass which will form the front is then placed carefully in position, propped up vertically from behind. The sides are attached by sealant in a similar way to the base and front, and then taped on the outside to the front. The final step is to fix the back of the tank in place, again taping this to the sides for extra support while the sealant is curing. A check should then be made to ensure that the whole unit is as square as possible, carrying out any slight adjustments at this stage.

After being left for a day, the tank can be finally sealed around its interior, taking care not to introduce bubbles of air into the seal. Strengthening bars, if necessary, are also inserted at this stage. Two days later, the tape around the corners can be removed, and the tank tested to ensure that it does not leak, whilst at the same time giving it a thorough washing-out. Although it is possible to cut away excess sealant with a sharp razor blade or modelling knife, this should be avoided if possible because the seal may be damaged accidentally in the process. As explained in the next chapter, such tanks when filled must always rest on a bed of polystyrene.

Other types of tank

Plastic tanks moulded as a complete unit are lighter than a glass design of similar dimensions. Unfortunately the plastic sides scratch very easily, and become unsightly, with debris and even algae sometimes accumulating in the depressions. The smaller rectangular designs are ideal for breeding tanks, however, while circular models are produced as goldfish tanks. These are free from the major, sometimes fatal disadvantage of the old glass goldfish bowl, which had a narrow neck. If these were filled to the top, the surface area was much reduced, so the fish could suffer from an oxygen deficiency, whereas when only half full, although this gave a bigger surface area, the volume of water available for swimming was much reduced and planting was also less successful. Such bowls should never be used, and rectangular tanks selected whenever possible.

Tank hoods

Hoods are manufactured in combination with specific sizes of tank. They serve to keep water loss through evaporation to a minimum, and help to reduce heating costs somewhat, since the air above the water is maintained at a relatively constant temperature. A hood will also prevent more active fish such as Oscars from jumping out of the tank, and reduces contamination of the water by household dust. If a hood of any kind is used with an angle-iron framed tank, small plastic clips should be purchased to prevent the two surfaces coming into direct contact, because condensation may drip on the iron frame, and cause it to rust along its upper surface. This occurs especially when just a sheet of glass is used as a cover.

Lighting

The majority of hoods also include space to fit an electric light to illuminate the tank, often with a raised surrounding area known as a reflector, which should spread the light evenly over the water surface. The usual incandescent domestic light bulb can be fitted, but these often have a relatively short lifespan under such conditions, as they are designed to be hung vertically, rather than horizontally. They also give out unwanted heat on to the surface of the water, and are relatively expensive to operate compared to fluorescent lighting.

Fluorescent tubes, produced in a range of sizes, are now used for illuminating aquariums. Those which emit light from the red and blue parts of the spectrum, thus closely imitating natural light, are of great value, being especially vital above a planted tank. the wavelengths of light produced by such tubes serve to encourage healthy plant growth and emphasize the colour of the fish to good advantage, with reds and blues particularly prominent. The light output from these tubes fades so it is not adviseable to use them beyond their recommended life.

The optimum amount of light which will be required is largely a matter of trial and error, as explained later, and the length of artificial illumination will need to be adjusted according to individual circumstances, to prevent excessive algal growth. The lighting can be controlled by a time switch, so that it will switch on and off automatically.

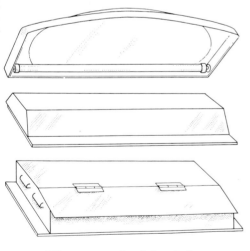

Three types of tank hood; the top one has a fluorescent tube fitted in place. A plastic splash cover, to protect the light, should be fitted below the hood. It will also prevent active fish from leaping up and burning themselves on the light.

Heaters and thermostats

The development of safe, accurate and reliable aquarium heaters controlled by thermostats is one of the major factors which has led to the huge growth in popularity of tropical fish-keeping. In the early years of the hobby, however, things were much harder, and the dedicated enthusiast had the choice of maintaining the temperature of water by means of oil lamps, which often filled the room with fumes, or gas jets, directed under the slate base of the tank.

The heater and thermostat can be purchased either as combined or separate units. The former arrangement is more straightforward, with less wiring involved, and is ideal for smaller tanks. In larger set-ups, however, where more than one heater is required, a separate thermostat in overall control may be preferable. External thermostats can be adjusted without disturbing the rest of the tank. Most thermostats are set around 25°C (75°F) following manufacture, but can be adjusted simply by a partial turn of a screw. Alterations to the setting may be necessary when treating an outbreak of disease, or when attempting to breed a particular species, for example.

The design of both heaters and thermostats is being rapidly updated, taking into account the benefits of silicon chip technology, which has revolutionized the whole electronics industry. The heating unit consists of an electric heating element encased in a glass tube, and these are available in various wattages, normally between 75 and 150 watts. The conventional thermostat has bi-metallic strips, which open and close depending on the water temperature, switching the heater on or off respectively. Unfortunately these contacts eventually lose their accuracy and may fuse together. The most modern units have no switches, and are thus more reliable and accurate, with a longer lifespan as well. A knowledgeable dealer will be able to advise on the best designs currently available, and it is often a false economy to purchase the cheapest model.

There is also a undertank option, in the form a very thin flexible pad, measuring about 0.625 cm ($\frac{1}{4}$ in) in thickness. Such heaters are unobtrusive, and transfer heat evenly through the aquarium, whether fitted beneath the base or at the back of the aquarium. They are available in various sizes, and have proved to be particularly valuable for large, aggressive fish which may attack and even break conventional units. Temperature control with a pad heater is again achieved by means of a thermostat.

What size heater? The size of heater required for a particular tank is calculated on the basis of 100 watts per 100 litres (22 gal) of water in the normal room, but in colder surroundings where there is no external heating, an additional 50 watts per 100 litres should be allowed. It is preferable not to have too powerful a heater for a given tank, because it will cause the thermostat to do more work, whereas a lower wattage heater will be on for a longer period to maintain the water temperature, but will cause less switching via the thermostat.

Thermometers The correct functioning of the heater and 'stat' must always be monitored by means of a thermometer. Various types are available, ranging from the traditional coloured-alcohol thermometer, mounted in a protective glass tube with a scale, which attaches by means of a rubber sticker to the inside surface of the tank. Circular models, with a pointer and scale sealed in a rubber casing are affixed in a similar way. These, however, perhaps because they are more bulky and have a reduced area of attachment, do not seem to stick in place as well as the tubular type.

Digital thermometers, first introduced to aquarists around 1977, have become very popular in a relatively short space of time. They adhere via a sticky backing to a glass surface on the outside of the aquarium. The water temperature within is transmitted to the cholesteric compound present in the flat strip constituting the thermometer, and registers visually in large figures on a coloured background. These thermometers are extremely accurate, being calibrated to within half a degree, but once positioned they cannot be moved successfully. In addition, young curious fingers can alter the temperature display easily by touching the strip. The lifespan of a digital thermometer is somewhat shorter than that of the conventional spirit type, but the ease of reading is an advantage.

Pumps

Aeration of the water in a tank primarily provides a means of circulating it, rather than introducing significant amounts of oxygen. Effective circulation of the water will help maintain a constant temperature throughout the tank. Air pumps for aquaria are marketed in a variety of sizes, and it is worth selecting a relatively expensive model, because cheaper designs are often more noisy when operating. Movement of water in the tank also ensures that debris and waste products from the fish can be removed via a filter, and pumps often have a dual role, forming part of a filtration system as well. A suitably powerful model should therefore be selected for a given tank.

The diaphragm pump is the type used almost universally by aquarists. It is operated by an electromagnet which vibrates up and down when current enters the device by a coil. In so doing, the magnet activates a diaphragm which draws air into the apparatus like a pair of bellows. The air then passes into the tank via tubing, with valves acting to even out the intermittent sucking effect of the

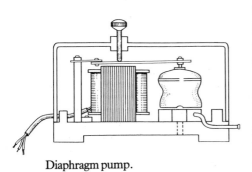
Diaphragm pump.

diaphragm, thus establishing a constant air flow. Some models also include a rheostat which indirectly controls the output of air by altering the input of power to the coil. As a result, the pump's action can be modified; it is quieter when less air is being drawn through it. The wattage of diaphragm pumps is extremely low, so the cost of running one round the clock, as will be necessary when it is connected to an undergravel filter, is virtually negligible.

A regular service of the pump, ensuring that all valves remain clean, and replacing the diaphragm at least annually, which is a relatively simple task, should ensure quiet trouble-free operation. Most pumps have a rubber base to reduce the noise resulting from vibration. If this is a particular problem, the unit can be placed on a pad of felt or similar material, which should help to quieten it, but it must never be covered in any way while operating because overheating will result, with the subsequent likelihood of fire.

Air-stones and air-lifts

The air pump is often connected up to air-stones that serve to break the air down into a constant stream of smaller bubbles, or to any of a series of tank ornaments such as clams or divers which emit bubbles of gas at regular intervals. An air-lift provides a refinement of this means of circulating water, and is comprised of a plastic tube set vertically in the tank to a level just below that of the surface. Air passes up the tube forcing water up above the surface level at the same time. This water can then be passed through a filter, or simply continue to circulate directly within the tank. Oxygenation at the surface is improved by this means.

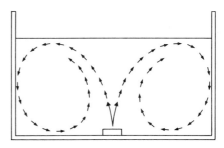

Air (diffuser) stone.

Filtration systems

The purpose of filtration is to remove waste matter from the tank that could otherwise build up and poison the tank's inhabitants. There are three basic systems of filtration available to aquarists for this purpose, and it is not uncommon for more than one to be used simultaneously. Indeed, biological filtration occurs naturally in established tanks, where bacteria present in the gravel degrade waste matter, and turn potentially toxic compounds such as ammonia and nitrite to nitrate, which can be taken up and utilized by the aquarium plants. For this system to work effectively, the bacteria must have adequate oxygen, and it is necessary to ensure that the tank is not overcrowded; nor should the fish be overfed, as the surplus simply increases the level of contamination. Mechanical filtration is a less complex system, where solid material is removed and retained when the water passes through a medium such as filter wool, which needs to be changed regularly to remain effective. This also applies to activated charcoal, used for chemical filtration

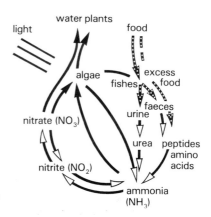

The nitrogen cycle:
Nitrite is a nitrogen compound which is formed in the aquarium by the breakdown of organic substances, such as fish faeces, urine, food remains and the dead parts of plants. Nitrite is only one of the stages in the breakdown of organic nitrogen to inorganic nitrate.

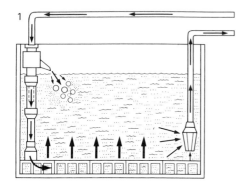

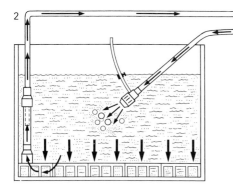

1 Substrate filtration with the water moving upwards through the substrate.

2 Substrate filtration with the water moving downwards through the substrate.

because of its large surface area. It absorbs dissolved organic waste products and other compounds present in the water into its many cracks and crevices. Filters used in aquaria rely on one or more of these means of filtration for their action.

Undergravel (U/G) or sub-gravel filters These filters, as their name suggests, are located on the floor of the aquarium, and are covered with gravel to a minimum depth of 7.5 cm (3 in). The gravel acts as the filter medium in this case, and so must be relatively coarse, approximately 3 mm ($\frac{1}{8}$ in), to ensure that it does not block the filter's pores. By means of an air pump, debris is drawn down with water through the gravel, where it is degraded by bacteria that form part of the nitrogen cycle. For maximum effectiveness, the filter plate should cover the whole of the floor of the aquarium, and although these filters are again produced in standard sizes, some can be cut to fit any size of tank.

Undergravel filters are relatively unobtrusive compared to other systems, and inexpensive. The air pump must be left on continuously, however, otherwise the beneficial aerobic bacteria will suffer accordingly, and the system breaks down as a result. These filters can become overworked, and so any accumulated debris on top of the gravel should be siphoned off each fortnight to lighten the load. Plants can also affect the efficiency of undergravel filters, as their roots may grow down through the pores and block them, also making it harder to thin out the vegetation without disturbing the whole tank. Growing plants in small plastic pots will help to overcome this difficulty.

Box filters Box filters are a common alternative to the undergravel filter, or may on occasions be used in conjunction with it. They fall into two categories, those which fit outside, and those which fit inside the tank. Although the latter type take up less space, often

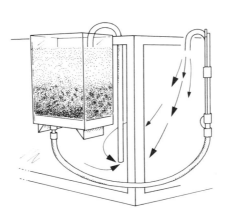

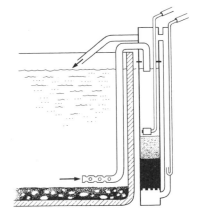

Left External filter worked by an air-lift. **Right** Air-lift system shown in detail.

fitting in the corner of a tank, they are somewhat harder to service, as will be necessary at regular intervals. Larger tanks certainly benefit from a filter of the external type, which is less restricted in size than its internal counterpart.

The box itself is usually a perspex container, filled with a combination of filter wool, activated carbon in the form of charcoal and sometimes gravel. A layer of charcoal is sandwiched between the two layers of nylon wool, with gravel at the bottom to weight down the container. Special wool and carbon are produced for these filters, and should always be used in preference to other similar materials, such as cotton wool, which is not recommended. Bone carbon is used because it sinks in water and has a better absorptive capacity than wood carbons. In some cases, filter wool is re-usable, while the carbon can be partially re-activated by heating. It is responsible for removing the toxic substances which are in solution, while the wool takes out solid debris from the water. Acid peat is also occasionally added to box filters, depending on the fish concerned and the state of the water.

These filters require an air pump to operate them, with air being introduced through a narrow-bore tube, and exiting through a broader outlet, drawing water out behind it. This in turn causes more water to enter the filter. In an external filter, water is drawn up out of the tank, passes through the filter bed and is then returned to the tank.

Power and polyfoam filters Many fish-keepers now rely on power filters, which can be either internal or external. The latter tend to be most suitable for larger tanks. These filters consist of two sections, and are operated independently of a box filter, because they contain a power unit.

This upper portion, called the impeller, is responsible for sucking in water through slits, which passes in turn through the cartridge, and out through a hole at the top of the filter. This is often positioned at the surface of the water, to assist with aeration. The filter medium in a power filter is usually a foam sponge. Although relatively expensive, power filters are especially useful for bigger, messier fish such as some cichlids.

Power filters are too strong for tanks housing young fry, but a polyfoam filter can be recommended for this situation. It fits inside the tank, being connected to an air pump here. This operates on a similar principle however, serving as a mechanical filter, with a population of aerobic bacteria developing here, enabling biological filtration to take place.

2 Setting up the Tank

The first step is to decide on the location of the tank in a room. The site chosen should be out of direct sunlight, because the aquarium's appearance will soon be spoilt by the resulting excessive algal growth, and the heat of the sun's rays is likely to affect the temperature of the water. Sudden changes of this nature are likely to prove harmful to the fishes themselves. For the same reason, tanks should never be placed in close proximity to room heaters, or near doors or windows where the temperature might fluctuate significantly. The background is not important, because scenic sheets which fit the back of the tank are available. It is also necessary to ensure that there is a power point for the electrical components of the tank within easy reach, and that overall the site is sufficiently accessible for maintenance purposes. Tanks positioned at eye-level are difficult to service, which will be necessary from time to time.

A new tank should be washed out thoroughly with salt water, and wiped round carefully with a clean cloth, just in case there are any minute slivers of glass present which could subsequently lodge, to ill-effect, in a fish's gills. No detergents or disinfectants should be used as these are likely to prove toxic if any residues remain after rinsing the tank out with cold water.

Once a large tank is full, it will be impossible to move it without removing the water. A litre of water weighs approximately 0.8 kg (1 gal of water weighs just over 8 lb). It is therefore vital that a secure base is chosen to support the tank, and whether or not a stand is used, a layer of polystyrene must be placed directly under the tank itself. This serves to counteract any unevenness in the surface, which would result in additional pressure on the glass of the tank, possibly causing it to leak.

The floor of the aquarium

Aquarium gravel is most commonly used on the floor of the tank. A fairly coarse grade, with individual particles about 3-4 mm (⅛ in) should be selected, especially when an undergravel filter is to be used, so that its pores do not become blocked. River sand is used in some tanks, but fine sand is not recommended, as the water will not be able to circulate effectively between the granules. Plant roots will also have difficulty penetrating a solid mass of sand.

When setting up a tank, the amount of gravel required can be calculated roughly on the basis of 1 kg per 4.5 litres (2 lb) per gallon) of water. Artificially-coloured gravel is popular, and available in an array of colours, but it is important to ensure that the dyeing agent remains fast, and will not come out into solution when placed in water. Although gravel obtained from aquarist shops has often been washed already, it should be rewashed to remove any remaining debris, and treated to ensure that no parasites or other harmful organisms could be introduced to the tank with it.

Washing is simply and effectively carried out using a plastic colander, with holes of a suitable size to retain the gravel or sand. This can then be transferred to a plastic bucket containing a solution of potassium permanganate (obtainable from a pharmacist), which will turn the water dark purple in colour. The gravel must be stirred up thoroughly several times over the course of a couple of days, and the washing procedure is then repeated until the emerging water is clear of any purple tinge. Although such treatment involves extra work, it is considerably easier to eliminate potential problems at this stage, rather than later, once the tank has actually been set up and the fishes introduced.

Plants in the aquarium

Although plastic plants are now available, and look extremely realistic in some cases, the provision of living plants in the aquarium will undoubtedly help to maintain the biological balance of the environment. They utilize the nitrate produced by bacteria from the breakdown of waste products in the tank, and are also involved in gas exchange, carrying out a process known as photosynthesis.

During the day, plants take up carbon dioxide from the water, which, in the presence of light, is used to produce carbohydrates for food, and in return they give off oxygen to the tank. At night, however, photosynthesis ceases and the situation is reversed, with the plants utilizing oxygen in minute quantities and releasing carbon dioxide. Some plants are better oxygenators than others, and this feature is directly related to the surface area of their leaves. Those with many small leaves, such as Java Moss, are better in this respect than broad-leaved species. The role of plants in maintaining a healthy aquatic environment was appreciated as long ago as 1850 when Robert Warrington gave details to the Chemical Society of how he was able to maintain goldfish in tanks without changing the water over several months if living plants were included from the outset.

Plastic plants It is not always possible to establish living plants in the aquarium, especially when the tank houses fish such as Jack

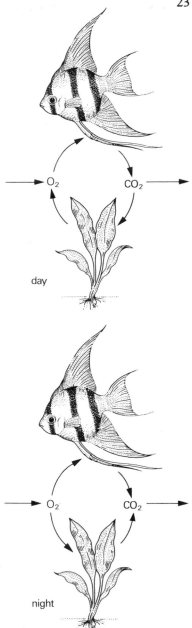

Gaseous exchange between water plants and fish.

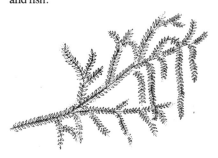

Jarva Moss (*Vesicularia dubyana*) is a good oxygenator in a tank.

Jack Dempsey Cichlid (*Cichlasoma octofasciatum*). This fish is destructive towards vegetation.

Dempsey cichlids, which will destroy vegetation. Plastic plants do have certain advantages over their living counterparts. They are not likely to introduce disease to the tank, and there are no problems in establishing them. Their plastic foliage does not deteriorate and thus detract from the overall appearance of the tank, yet like genuine plants, they provide cover for the fish. The problem of algal growth developing in the tank is more likely to arise with plastic plants, however, because there will be an excess of nitrate circulating in the water which would normally be utilized by aquatic vegetation.

The choice of plants A very wide range of plants is available for the aquarium and these may be sold either individually, or as mixed collections for various sizes of tank. It is important to have some details about a particular type of plant before acquiring it, so that its suitability for, and place in, the tank can be assessed in advance.

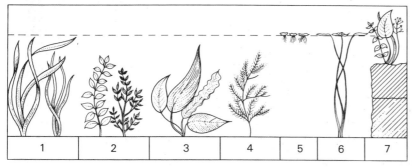

Water-plant types:
1 with strap-like leaves; **2** with coarse or mossy leaves; **3** with long stalks; **4** with feathery leaves; **5** floating plants; **6** rooted plants with floating leaves; **7** marsh plants.

Indeed, not all plants offered would normally be totally submerged throughout the year. Many cryptocornes, or 'Crypts', of which over fifty-five species are recognized, are really marshland plants, only totally immersed in water during the wet season, for two months or so out of the whole year. This genus is confined to south-east Asia. These plants are relatively slow-growing in the aquarium, and in the natural state, remain inactive when submerged. The various species occur in several colours, ranging from bluish-green in the case of *Cryptocoryne affinis* to reddish in some strains of *C. wendtii*. One of the smaller members of the group is *C. nevillii*, which reaches a size of only about 7.5 cm (3 in), whereas *C. ciliata* can grow to 60 cm (2 ft), making it rather large for the average aquarium. It does well, however, in slightly brackish water.

Successful cultivation of cryptocornes requires a minimum of disturbance, and moving them will prove a definite set-back to their growth. They tend not to like excessive light, or hard water, but adapt well to the temperature of a tropical tank, providing it

Cryptocoryne affinis.

Echinodorus cordifolius.

Elodea densa. Plants such as this can be bought as cuttings and anchored into the substrate, where they will take root.

does not exceed 27°C (80°F). Flowering is rare, although *C. griffithii* is most likely to yield results in this direction.

The genus *Echinodorus* contains the aquarium plants which are often known as 'Amazon Sword Plants'. Although the majority of species occur in Central and South America, others are known from the Caribbean, as well as Europe and North Africa. Those commonly sold as aquarium plants range in size from about 7.5 cm (3 in) in the case of *E. tenellus* up to about 40 cm (16 in) for *E. bleheri*. Although many have elongated leaves, those of *E. cordifolius* are heart-shaped. Water which is relatively soft suits *Echinodorus* well, and these plants are easily propagated by means of their runners, or from small plantlets which develop on the stems. They are very suitable for tanks where the fish have a tendency to destroy vegetation, because their tough fronds offer good protection, and they are fast-growing by nature.

Another strong plant, which is also extremely adaptable, thriving even in coldwater aquaria, is *Elodea densa*. It is widely available, and soon roots readily from cuttings. *Elodea* thrives especially in well-lit surroundings in hard water and so is not really compatible with the various cryptocornes. *Elodea*, with its high lime requirement may actually serve to soften hard water. Two other forms, *E. canadensis* (Canadian pondweed) and *E. callitrichoides* (Chilian pondweed), should only be used in coldwater surroundings, as they will not adapt well to the warmth of a tropical tank.

Hygrophila polysperma, a native of India, is a highly versatile plant, unaffected by the condition of the water. It can adjust to temperatures ranging from 12°-30°C (54°-86°F) and parts are easily rooted. Planted in bunches, it shows to good effect against darker *Cryptocoryne* species, and provides ample cover for the fish once established. *H. difformis* is a more demanding member of the genus, preferring soft water and good light.

Ludwigia natans also appreciates bright surroundings, but does not thrive in tanks where the water temperature is much above 25°C (77°F). Cuttings grow readily and may be required if the lower leaves are lost, often as the result of inadequate light. *Myriophyllum*, which has much finer leaves, is very similar to *Ludwigia* in its requirements. *Nomaphila stricta* also does well in good light, but can stand a higher range of temperatures, between 22°-30°C (72°-86°F). It grows relatively fast under suitable conditions, but often proves a favourite food with any snails present in the tank.

Various members of the genus *Sagittaria* are used to decorate aquaria, and out of these, *S. latifola* is perhaps most commonly seen. *Sagittaria* does well across a fairly broad temperature range, and will not require excessive lighting. Light exposure can, however, affect the colour of these plants, as is also the case with members of other genera. *S. subulata* for example, becomes reddish when exposed to a high intensity of illumination.

Vallisneria, which has a similar appearance to certain *Sagittarias* is often found in planted aquaria, located towards the back of the tank. *V. spiralis* can reach a size of 60 cm (2 ft), and the subspecies *V. s. torta* has more twisted leaves than the nominate race. The giant form, *V. gigantea*, should only be acquired for large and deep set-ups, as its leaves are likely to grow to at least 1 m (3 ft) in length. Distinct male and female plants of this species are recognized. Rooted plants should be set with their crowns above the substrate.

Floating plants While the plants discussed previously live rooted in the substrate of the tank, there is another group which naturally occur on the surface of the water, giving areas of shade beneath them. The Underwater Banana Plant (*Nymphoides aquatica*), named after its tuberous roots which resemble a cluster of the fruit, can either be allowed to float freely, or be planted in the substrate. It prefers slightly acid water, but, in common with all members of this group, if the conditions are too favourable, its foliage may completely smother the surface of the tank, unless it is held in check.

The attractive Water Sprite prefers an uncovered tank. The form known as *Ceratopteris cornuata* can grow to a size of 50 cm (20 in) if given adequate space in relatively soft water with a temperature between 20° and 30°C (68°-86°F). Its dangling roots are a favourite retreat of young fry. Another species *C. thalictroides*, known as Sumatra Fern is also quite often available.

Salvinia auriculata is more suitable for the smaller tropical tank, by virtue of its size, with leaves only about 1.25 cm (½ in) long. It is a rootless fern which thrives in a well-lit environment, and is favoured by bubble-nest builders, including the Fighting Fish, to lend support to their nests. Although *Salvinia* produces spores, these do not mature in the aquarium, and spread occurs by pieces breaking off from the main plant. Another small tropical American floating plant often seen in aquaria is *Limnobium stoloniferum*, which requires soft water conditions. Propagation in this case is from runners.

Summary While this section has dealt with a selection of the most commonly-available and easily-grown aquatic plants, it is not a comprehensive review of this aspect of the hobby. There are now several books available which are devoted solely to the topic of aquarium plants, and further reference should be made to these for detailed information on a particular species. In addition, there are specialist aquatic nurseries where a wide range of water plants can be obtained, along with advice on their subsequent care. Such nurseries often advertize in fish-keeping journals, and generally operate a mail-order business, as well as catering for callers.

Ludwigia natans.

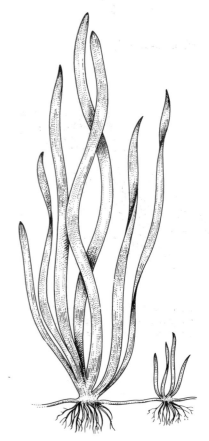

Vallisneria spiralis.

Haplochromis euchilus. A cichlid which uses its thick lips to strip algae off rocks.

Planting principles

An overall plan for the tank should have been worked out, with plants and rockwork included in the design. Taller plants such as *Vallisneria* and *Sagittaria* are typically located towards the back of the tank, with a Sword Plant positioned in the centre. Smaller plants such as *C. nevilli* are found in the foreground.

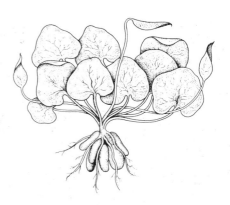

Nymphoides aquatica.

Having acquired the plants, it is advisable to wash them off thoroughly in a salt solution, because they can introduce pests such as *Planaria* into the aquarium. A solution made up with 31 g (1 oz) of salt per 4.5 litres (1 gal) of water will be adequate for this purpose. They will then need to be rinsed off and have any dead leaves removed before being placed in the tank.

The floor covering of the tank is not as significant for plants as may be thought. Those which are genuinely adapted for life in water take most of their nutrients directly from their aquatic environment, and not via their roots, which merely provide anchorage in the substrate. There are many different recommendations for planting media, to take into account the differing requirements of the various plants, but the majority prove fairly adaptable. It is possible to plant them all individually in small pots, to cater for their individual preferences, but this detracts from the overall appearance of the aquarium, and is not strictly necessary. The use of pots can be advantageous in a tank where the occupants will uproot vegetation. In addition, the root system, and thus the growth, of plants such cryptocornes, will not be damaged by later movement if they are set in pots. A mixture of loam and acid peat covered with the aquarium substrate should be used in such pots.

Rockwork

In the same way that plants provide cover, food and breeding habitats, so rockwork in the tank can also benefit the fish. Some cichlids may be induced to breed by the presence of flat stones or sunken flowerpots, while certain catfish, for example, will feed on algae growing on rockwork and often hide beneath it. Only hard, non-soluble rocks, such as granite, slate or sandstone should be included in the tank, however, because they will not affect the water's hardness. Limestone rocks contain calcium carbonate, which will slowly dissolve into the water in the presence of dissolved carbon dioxide, causing the water to increase significantly in hardness. This will prove detrimental to the vast majority of fish and plants.

Although suitable aquarium stone can be purchased, it is also possible to collect attractive rocks from many places, such as river beds. If in doubt as to whether a particular rock contains limestone, there is a simple test which can be carried out to detect the presence of this chemical. When a few drops of hydrochloric or sulphuric acid are applied carefully to the rock's surface, any sign of effervescence reveals the presence of calcium carbonate. Rockwork intended for the aquarium should be scrubbed off thoroughly in salt water, and rinsed before being placed in the tank.

Wood

Wood in the aquarium can be decorative, and may form a significant feature of spawning tanks. Willow root, for example, can often be used to induce members of the genus *Aphyosemion* to spawn, the eggs of these tooth carps being laid in amongst the individual strands. Alder, birch or oak are also suitable woods for use in aquaria.

Once again, the first step must be to sterilize the wood completely, and this can be achieved by placing it in an old, large saucepan complete with a lid. The wood should then be boiled for a couple of hours, ensuring that it remains covered with water. After a final scrubbing and thorough rinse, it is ready for use in the tank.

Both artificial wood and rockwork are now available. These are lighter than real pieces and often prove more satisfactory.

Water: hardness and acidity

The relative hardness of water is influenced by its source. In areas where tap water contains significant proportions of dissolved calcium and magnesium salts, obtained from the rocks which it has come into contact with, it is described as being 'hard'. Rainwater on the other hand, is relatively pure, being free from such salts, and is therefore referred to as 'soft'. The degree of hardness is measured on the German °DH scale, with one unit being equivalent to 10mg of calcium, in the form of calcium oxide, which is present in 1 litre (1.75 pt) of water. Most fish, living in areas of water swollen by rain, prefer relatively soft water, although there are exceptions, such as the Rift Valley cichlids, which occur in the isolated lakes formed in this volcanic region. The following table gives an indication of the relative hardness of water, based on the DH scale. Distilled water, being pure, has a zero reading.

°DH	Water
0-4	Very soft
5-8	Soft
9-12	Moderately hard
13-18	Harder
19-30	Hard
30+	Very hard

Note: Other hardness scales exist, with the UK° Clark scale being equivalent to 14.3 mg/litre of calcium carbonate. The corresponding °DH figure is 17.9 mg/l, while in the USA, the

°hardness scale is based on 1 mg/l, or 1 part per million (ppm) of calcium carbonate. It can be easier to stick to this ppm figure.

Hardness of water can be further sub-divided into permanent and temporary hardness. Permanent hardness results from the presence of sulphates, and unlike temporary hardness, cannot be removed by boiling. Temporary hardness, sometimes expressed as the KH reading, is significant because it can act as a buffer in the water to overcome minor pH changes.

The pH value is a measurement of the relative acidity of the water in the tank. The scale of pH readings can extend from 0 to 14, with 7 being neutral. When below this figure, water conditions are said to be acid, whereas above 7, they are alkaline. Most tapwater varies between 7 and 8, and this is suitable to maintain some fish without additional treatment. Discus and killifish typically require more acid conditions, however, whereas the Rift Valley cichlids come from alkaline waters. In addition, the pH is often of vital importance for the successful breeding of other fish, such as barbs, which require soft, acid water. The individual requirements of particular groups are considered later, in the section devoted to the fish themselves. All fish are very sensitive to any sudden alterations in the pH value of their surroundings, and a fluctuation of more than one unit in a day is likely to have fatal consequences. Gradual adaptation over quite a wide range is, however, possible.

Testing water conditions When assessing the degree of hardness, or the pH value, of a sample of water, the simplest means is to acquire the appropriate test kits available from aquarist dealers. These are quite straightforward to use, and often more reliable than other methods, such as litmus paper, used for pH measurements. A local dealer is likely to have similar water conditions, and this may be advantageous when buying the fish.

Alteration of hardness and pH On occasions, it may be necessary to adjust these levels for particular fish. If the water is too hard, this can be overcome by adding distilled water in the correct proportions to attain the desired degree of softness. For example, knowing that the tap water is 16°DH and aiming to obtain very soft water with a DH reading of 2°, fourteen parts of distilled water must be added to two parts of tap water as shown. Boiling will remove the carbonate component of hardness, (and also lower the ability of the water to effectively neutralize pH changes, as its buffering capacity is compromised), but this alteration is only temporary, because carbon dioxide dissolved in the water will gradually regenerate the carbonate. The addition of calcium sulphate to the tank will increase the hardness of the water if this is necessary, but such alterations should always be checked over a period of time, before the fish are added to the tank.

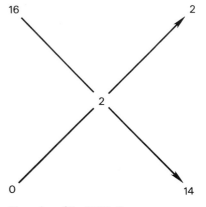

Alteration of the °DH of water.

As mentioned previously, limestone rocks in the aquarium will increase the hardness of the water, and they will also raise the pH. The simplest and safest means of lowering the pH value is to add peat to the tank. This is simply done by including aquarium peat in a box filter, with the water circulating through it. Alternatively, peat stitched into a nylon bag and placed in the tank, working on the basis of a handful of peat per 4.5 litres (1 gal) of water, will also serve to soften the water over the course of a day or so. The peat will need replacing every fortnight to maintain its action, usually when the filter itself is changed.

Establishing the tank

After the tank has been placed in position, and the undergravel filter added, if one is to be used, the gravel can be tipped carefully into the aquarium. This should be sloped down towards the front so that subsequently any debris will be evident. The thicker layer of gravel at the back of the tank also affords a deeper substrate for plant roots, and serves to partially disguise pots if these are used.

It is preferable to fill the tank at least half-full of water before putting the plants and other tank decorations in place. Water from a cold tap is safer, because in some cases, the concentration of copper dissolved from pipes in the heating system into the water itself may subsequently prove toxic to the fish. By pouring the water carefully on to a plate located on the surface of the gravel there should be little disturbance to the actual gravel base itself.

Then working to the scheme previously devised, the plants can be set in place, starting at the back of the tank. There are planting tools available to facilitate this task. In the case of plants with long roots, such as *Cryptocoryne* and *Vallisneria* species, they must be planted in a correspondingly deep hole. Spacing between individual plants depends on the type concerned. A minimum area of 5 sq cm (2 sq in) should be allowed, with a gap of 15 cm (6 in) separating plants which reach a larger size. Cuttings are often planted in small groups, each weighed down individually with a suitable stone, until they have rooted. It is very important that the plants are kept moist after purchase until they are back in water, because their leaves may otherwise be damaged by desiccation, and their appearance subsequently spoilt.

Rocks and wood can then be added, taking care to leave sufficient swimming area for the fish themselves. The rockwork must be firm, especially in tanks for larger fish, such as Oscars, because they may dislodge unstable rocks with serious consequences, and also injure themselves on any rough, exposed edges. If wood is to be used, it must remain saturated, and thus below the water level rather than floating on the surface. This can be achieved by wedging it soundly with rockwork. It is also possible to encourage vegetation to develop on the wood. A plant which looks most attractive when growing on sunken wood or roots is Java Fern (*Microsorium pteropus*).

Electrical matters

The electrical components of the aquarium can be wired up and placed in position next. If in any doubt about the wiring, advice should be sought from a qualified electrician. It is possible to use a junction box for the wiring so that all the units feed into the mains supply via a single plug, which is safer and also dispenses with the need for adaptors. When using a combined heater and thermostat, the unit should be fixed with its rubber suckers onto the back of the tank, keeping the thermostat higher than the heating unit, so that it is not positioned horizontally. Under no circumstances should such units be switched on out of the water or buried in the substrate. An independent thermostat must always be located as far away as possible from the heater, preferably at the other end of the tank, with the thermometer placed close to the thermostat on the front panel where it can be easily read.

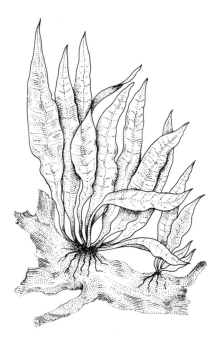

Microsorium pteropus.

The air pump will need to be included in the circuitry, and fixed in with the filter and air-stone as appropriate. The system can then be tested, and the water left to warm up, which is likely to take several hours. Various alarm systems are now available to detect any electrical failures in the heating system, and it is worth adding one of these to the tropical tank.

Toxic chemicals

You cannot add the fish to the tank as soon as the water temperature has stabilized at the desired level, because the level of chlorine present in the tap water will poison them. As little as 0.1 mg of chlorine per litre (1.75 gal) has proved toxic to fish. A special dechlorinator and water conditioner to make the tank water safe for the fish is useful. Alternatively, leaving the water to stand for at least a day should dissipate the chlorine. A fresh start product, which will help to seed the filter with beneficial bacteria can also be recommended, in the case of a new aquarium.

Another chemical, produced from waste products in the newly established tank, which is likely to be detrimental to the fishes' health is ammonia. At this stage, there are no established bacteria to break it down to relatively harmless nitrate. A recent advance to overcome the problem is the use of Zeolite, which is a natural resin, produced in sachets to fit in the filtration system or in the tank itself. This compound effectively absorbs ammonia from the water, and can be re-used repeatedly simply by immersing it overnight in a cup of salt water.

Introducing the fish

If possible, the tank should be set up about a week before the fish are introduced into it. This will give the plants time to become well established, and the filter bed to become active.

It is much easier to purchase all the fish for the tank simultaneously, preferably from the same source. The addition of new arrivals to an established tank can be fraught with problems. Fish are usually sold in plastic bags, containing a relatively small amount of their tank water, but a large volume of air to ensure that they have sufficient oxygen for their journey. This is why a dealer often blows up the bag before sealing it: contrary to popular belief, our lungs only extract a proportion of the atmospheric oxygen inhaled, with a significant quantity being exhaled again at the end of each breath.

The temperature of the water in the bag will have fallen during transit, and once at home, the bag should first be floated in the tank water for a period of time to enable the water temperature to even out, before releasing the fish. This gives them an opportunity to adjust gradually to the fluctuations in temperature which they have experienced, and thus reduces the stress on them. The bag can then be gently inverted into the water, allowing the fish out into their new environment.

3 Maintenance

The fish will take a while to adjust to their move, and should be watched closely for any signs of illness, which is especially likely to develop at this stage. Some, such as Dwarf Rainbow Cichlids (*Pelamatochromus kribensis*), may undergo a loss of colour at first, but this is only a temporary change.

Feeding

In the wild, fish eat a range of foods, and their diet is often influenced by seasonal availability. The Bermuda Angelfish (*Holacanthus bermudensis*), for example, feeds largely on plant matter during the winter and spring, becoming carnivorous in the summer. Certain species are adapted to feed on particular foods. In Lake Victoria, where over 170 different species of cichlid occur, some strip algae off rocks using their chisel-like teeth, whereas others with a wide gape are predatory in their feeding habits. A few fish, such as some South American characoids, actually consume the scales of neighbouring fish, feeding off their sides.

Feeding fish in the aquarium is not difficult, and there is now a wide range of prepared foods available, containing all the ingredients necessary to keep the fish in good health. There is also no risk of introducing disease to the tank occupants using such foods. Most ranges contain a basic staple diet, which can be augmented

Haplochromis polystigma. One of the predatory cichlids, certainly not recommended for inclusion in any community tank.

with other products such as a conditioning food. It is preferable to select one brand, and use the various items of the range as recommended. Colour foods, to improve the coloration of certain fish such as Flame Tetras (*Hyphessobrycon flammeus*) are also now available, as well as diets specifically intended for fry, and particular fish such as guppies.

These diets are manufactured in the form of flakes and tablets, which contain very little water compared to natural foods. Certain fish, such as discus and angelfish, can be tamed sufficiently to eat out of the hand, especially when feeding takes place at regular times each day.

It is vital that fish are only offered a relatively small amount of food, which should be consumed within minutes of being placed in the tank. One of the most common errors of the novice aquarist is overfeeding. Excess food will pollute the tank, and may harm the fish. Their digestive systems are not adapted to eating one large meal daily because in the wild, they feed throughout the day. Several small meals are therefore recommended, with the food being introduced in a feeding ring, which floats on the surface, thus retaining the flakes in one place. Flake food will slowly sink, however, and will then be consumed by the bottom-feeders, such as catfish. Tablet diets are more commonly used for such fish, and they can nibble pieces off a block.

Livefoods Livefoods fed to fish can be divided into two categories, those invertebrates which occur naturally in water, and those which are cultivated or collected from other environments. Although fish undoubtedly enjoy such items on their menu, aquatic livefoods present a potential health hazard, as a range of other creatures, as well as disease, may be accidentally introduced with them. Aquatic beetles for example, will attack all fish, and *Hydra*, which is related to the jellyfishes, can destroy large numbers of fry in a short period of time by means of its stinging tentacles. Furthermore, *Hydra* may at first sight be confused with *Cyclops*, which is a crustacean actually used as livefood for fish. These two creatures can be distinguished by their movements, as *Cyclops* swims whereas *Hydra*, with its flexible body, contracts down to escape detection at a hint of danger.

Two of the most popular aquatic livefoods for fish are *Daphnia*, also known as water fleas, and tubifex worms, both of which are commonly stocked by aquarist shops. Daphnia are sold in plastic bags full of water, and before purchasing them a check should be made to ensure that a significant proportion are alive and moving. In any bag, a number will be dead, and if not used immediately, the bag should be kept cool to avoid larger losses. These crustaceans are not, in fact, related to fleas, but have a similar shape and jerky motion.

When feeding daphnia to fish, a special set of sieves should be acquired so that the water can be filtered off from the bag. This helps to reduce the risk of introducing pests present in the water, as they may be more visible in the sieve, but more significantly, pouring the water containing the daphnia into the tank will certainly upset the temperature, and perhaps the pH and °DH values of the water as well. As a source of livefood, daphnia are said to improve colour as well as having a laxative effect on the fish.

Tubifex worms are found in fairly unsavoury surroundings, typically in the vicinity of sewage outlets, where they feed on the effluent. In London, tubifex occur right in the centre of the city, down river in the Thames from Chelsea, and their collection is licenced by the Port of London Authority. Thorough cleansing through running water decreases contamination, but some aquarists are very doubtful about using tubificid worms for their fish.

Catfish, such as the Leopard Corydoras (*Corydoras julii*) shown here, often feed near the bottom of a tank.

The worms can be kept alive for a period of time out of water, with measured quantities usually being sold wrapped in paper. On arrival home, they should be transferred to a container positioned under a dripping tap, to ensure a constant flow of water over them. They will soon die if left in a jam jar simply covered in water, unless it is changed very frequently. Tubifex should be offered to the fish in a special feeder, which is shaped like a nozzle, and prevents the whole mass from sinking to the bottom of the tank at once.

There are various other aquatic livefoods which can be fed to fish, such as gnat larvae found during the summer months in stagnant pools and waterways. The safest method of obtaining these is to attract the adult gnats by leaving a clean bucket containing aged tap water outside. They will then lay their eggs, and once the larvae hatch, these can be collected by sieving.

Non-aquatic livefood There are always likely to be potential problems over the collection and storage of the previously mentioned invertebrates, and shop supplies are not always reliable. Suitable alternatives can be cultured or obtained with little effort to overcome such difficulties. Whiteworm (*Enchytraeus*) is typical of this group. A culture is easily established in a disused plastic ice-cream container, half-filled with damp soil, with moistened bread on top. The bread should only be given in relatively small amounts, enough to last the worms for a couple of days, with any surplus then being removed and replaced. On occasions, the bread may have turned red, indicating the presence of a bacterium, *Bacillus prodigiosus*, but this causes no harm. Mites also contaminate some cultures and likewise have no adverse effects on the worms or fish.

The whiteworm culture may be covered with a lid, perforated with ventilation holes to keep it dark and to prevent the soil drying out. Regular spraying of the soil surface will be necessary, but it should never be waterlogged. Several colonies can be set up simultaneously using worms purchased from an aquarist dealer, and maintained in cool surroundings, with a temperature between 15° and 20°C (58°-68°F). After a month or so, depending on the conditions, whiteworms can be harvested on a regular basis. They are easily collected from beneath chunks of bread using forceps and can then be washed off and separated from the substrate in a saucer of water, or sieved. The worms range in size from about 0.5-1.25 cm (¼-½ in), and may need to be chopped for feeding to small fish. Specific foods for young fry are considered in the next chapter.

Earthworms are freely available in most gardens, especially during periods of wet weather, when they are drawn to the surface, but they are also sold in many angling shops. A worm trap can be set up to avoid digging haphazardly in a garden, by simply laying damp hessian sacking on a shaded piece of ground, which has been well-watered previously, and then adding some vegetable matter under the sacking to attract the worms. Worms found around manure heaps, especially the Brandling which has a noticeably 'ringed' appearance, should be avoided. After collection, the worms will need to be transferred to a suitable container as for whiteworm, but lined with damp moss and grass, for several days so they can empty their gut contents. Smaller whole worms are often useful in tempting reticent individuals, such as Siamese Fire Eels (*Mastacembelus erythrotaenia*) to feed when placed directly in front of them. These eels have poor eyesight, and detect food with their nose.

Another commercially-available livefood which has become somewhat more expensive recently, is the redworm (*Dendrobina rubica*), mainly used as fishing bait. These worms can be purchased in pre-packed tubs containing a sterile medium, and then fed directly. They tend to be somewhat smaller than earthworms, which is an advantage as they may not need to be cut up for feeding. When kept in a temperature of 5°-10°C (40°-50°F), the supply will last for several weeks, as long as the medium is not allowed to dry out.

Fruit flies (*Drosophila*) are an ideal livefood for surface-feeding fish. A culture can easily be started and maintained using old banana skins in jam jars which are covered with muslin. When provided with a sugar mixture, and kept warm, these flies breed freely, and can be tipped out onto the water's surface. The wingless mutant form is preferable as fish food, because it cannot fly.

Mealworms are another livefood which can be offered to larger fish such as cichlids, and have a high protein content. Their hard outer covering of chitin is a deterrent to some fish, and it is preferable to use moulting soft-skinned individuals, which are white rather than yellowish in colour. Mealworms can be kept in bran, to which a vitamin and mineral powder has been added, along with slices of apple on the surface, and housed in a covered container as suggested previously.

As a change from livefood, ox heart can be fed with considerable benefit. Studies undertaken in California using guppies have shown that their lifespan could be increased by up to 50 per cent when feeding ox heart every other day. It is simply prepared by dicing the meat into small pieces, taking care to remove any fat and remains of blood vessel walls. The resulting chunks should be placed in a liquidizer and blended to the consistency of porridge. Discrete spoonfuls can then be placed on clean plastic bags in a deep freeze until they are hard, and stored for later use. One or two such balls are removed and thawed at room temperature to provide a single feed for the guppies. The major disadvantage of feeding heart is that it soils the water, and cleanliness of the tank assumes greater significance. The fish void whitish droppings on a diet of heart, and this is quite normal.

Other meat products can be fed to fish, typically the larger more carnivorous species such as cichlids. Canned dog food is often acceptable, but it is important that pieces are cut up very small so the fish cannot choke on them. In addition, if the tin is already opened and thus stored in a refrigerator, the meat must not be fed directly, but allowed to warm up at room temperature first. Dried dog food can also be used, providing it is well soaked before being offered to the fish.

Freeze-dried livefood The technique of freeze-drying has revolutionized the availability of livefoods for the aquarist previously dependent on local supplies, but although the process itself was well-known at the beginning of the nineteenth century, it has only been widely used during recent years. The livefood, such as tubifex, is prepared by freezing, to convert all the water present into ice, and this is then removed by drying without actually heating the product. As a result, it retains its flavour and smell, and thus appeal to the fish. For the aquarist, a freeze-dried product can be stored indefinitely in the home and its nutritional quality will not deteriorate. Tubifex is conveniently packed in small blocks, which float on the surface of the water when first added to the tank, attracting the fish to them.

A drawback of the freeze-drying technique is that any bacteria originally present in the livefood itself will not have been destroyed. This has been overcome by gamma irradiation of such foodstuffs, which are then reconstituted by the addition of vitamins destroyed by the radiation itself. These products are sold in foil packets from specialist outlets, and have to be kept refrigerated.

Vegetable intake Many fish take a proportion of vegetable matter as part of their diet, if given the opportunity. Certain aquatic plants, such as Java Moss are particularly attractive to fish for food, and they will eat the tops off the growing shoots. Algae in the tank are another source of food, often favoured by mollies, loaches and *Synodontis* catfish amongst others. In a newly-established tank there will be no algal growth, and as an alternative, boiled lettuce or spinach should be provided. Duckweed (*Lemna* species), which floats on the water surface, can be included in tanks for cichlids that eat vegetable matter, since they will often feed on this plant. Boiled oatmeal, which contains a significant amount of protein, is another alternative food.

Observing feeding behaviour It is important to note whether the fish are all eating, because loss of appetite is often a sign of impending illness. Some fish, such as angelfish and discus, can lose their appetites for no apparent reason, and may need to be tempted by a change in diet. Any fish which persist in spitting out food should be removed from the tank, as they are likely to have an intestinal complaint.

In the communal tank, feeding time is the time when bullying is most likely to be evident, and slower, shyer fish must be allowed an opportunity to feed unmolested. There is no need to worry over the feeding ability of Blind Cave Characins (*Astyanax jordani*) even in a tank alongside other fish, as they are often amongst the first to find food. They have developed an acute sense of smell to compensate for their lack of vision and only when offered daphnia are they possibly at a disadvantage.

Algal growth

Although the presence of algae in a tank can be of benefit to the fish by providing a readily-available source of food, they may also spoil the appearance of the tank if their growth is not kept in check. There are over 18,000 different species of alga known, some of which live in suspension in the water, causing it to be cloudy while others prefer to colonize rockwork and sides of the tank. These minute plants also occur in a range of colours, from brown and green to blue. Those found in aquariums are often introduced with livefoods, plants or even the fish themselves.

The major predisposing factor to excessive growth of green algae in a tank is too much illumination, and aquaria which are exposed to sunlight as well as artificial light often suffer severely from an explosion of the algal population. A maximum of eight hours total artificial lighting per day is sufficient when no sunlight falls on the tank, and this should be reduced accordingly if the aquarium is in an environment which is naturally well-lit.

In the face of a severe rise in algal contamination, the fish themselves may start showing signs of ill-thrift. As with plants, algae utilize oxygen from the water at night, and in sufficient numbers may deplete the supply so that the fish become starved of this vital gas. In addition, algae may also poison fish directly by liberating toxins which accumulate in the water.

When attempting to clear a tank of excessive algae, it may be necessary to transfer the fish elsewhere, and clean the tank thoroughly. Hot water alone, with a temperature in excess of 80°C (176°F) will kill algae, so all parts of the tank, including the gravel, should be left to stand in water for a quarter of an hour or so. This treatment should then be repeated, because algal spores are quite resistant to destruction. The tank itself should be filled cautiously with hot water, and then wiped round and rinsed. It is well-worth doing the job thoroughly once, rather than having to repeat it, and this will also be much less disturbing for the fish. The aquarium should then be set up again as before, but in a different location if necessary, or with the amount of illumination reduced. Overfeeding of plants may also contribute to excessive algal growth.

Tank hygiene

Regular cleaning of the tank on a limited basis is all that is generally needed to keep algal growth in check. The sides of the tank can be easily cleaned from the outside using a magnetic scraper. The cleaning pad complete with magnet is introduced at the top of the tank above water-level and held in place by another magnet on the outer surface. The sides of the aquarium can then be cleaned individually by moving the magnet outside the tank up and down the glass, which draws the scraper with it, and causes the minimum disturbance to the fish in the process. It is also possible to acquire cleaning pads on long handles which perform a similar function. Special care is needed when cleaning the sides of plastic tanks since these scratch very easily, and their appearance suffers as a result.

Algae will also colonize filters and connecting tubing, which can be cleaned with the appropriate set of brushes. It bears repetition here that the brushes should not be washed out in disinfectants or detergents at all, because residues are likely to be introduced to the tank when they are next used, with potentially fatal consequences.

Particularly stubborn deposits of algae can be removed directly by means of a clean razor blade (although not recommended for plastic tanks) or a paper tissue. Rubber gloves should always be worn if there is any risk of contaminating the aquarium water with chemicals present on the hand. Brown algae, which is suggestive of too little lighting, comes off as distinct scrapings which will then need to be syphoned out of the tank, whereas green algae is softer and adheres well to paper tissues. Various aquarium cleaners are marketed to suck out such debris, but a suitable length of flexible rubber tubing, such as that used for bunsen burners is quite adequate.

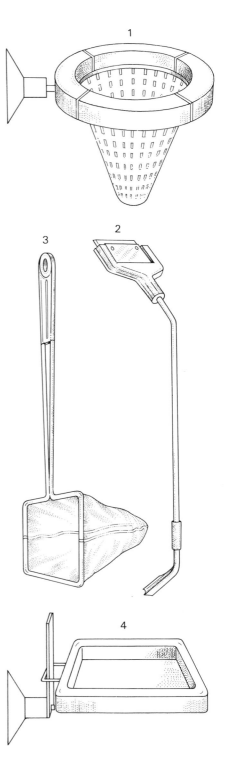

Useful tank equipment:
1 Tubifex worm feeder;
2 scraper for removing algae;
3 fish net;
4 feeding ring.

The tubing is filled with aged water from a plant watering can, and then both ends are covered with a finger from each hand. One end is then placed in the tank, and the finger released, while the other is transferred to a bucket placed on the floor below the level of the tank. Once the finger over this end of the tube is lifted, water will flow into the bucket. Apart from removing debris, a partial water change can be undertaken every month or so by this means. Up to one-third of the water in the tank is replaced with fresh 'aged' water, and can be used subsequently to good effect for household plants because of its relatively high nitrate content.

Snails

Some aquarists favour the presence of snails in aquaria, pointing out that they will consume algae and other debris which otherwise would accumulate in the tank. The opposite view regards snails not as beneficial, but as potential sources of problems, citing the damage caused to growing vegetation and further soiling of the tank as examples. Undeniably, snails do provide another focus of interest in the aquarium and can reproduce successfully in it. Young snails often fall victim to carnivorous fish, and a population explosion is unlikely to occur, as their number will be kept in check naturally.

Apple Snails belonging to the genus *Ampullaria* have unusual breeding habits. They actually lay their eggs above the water surface, and these must be kept moist if they are to hatch successfully. This can be achieved by positioning an air-stone close by, which gives them a light spray, but prevents them from becoming saturated. The Mystery Snail (*A. cuprina*) is the most desirable member of the genus for the aquarist because it will not destroy vegetation as much as other Apple Snails. They feed on a range of items including algae and tubifex.

Ramshorn Snails (*Planorbis* species) have a distinctly flat, coiled appearance, and are sometimes introduced accidentally on vegetation. The Red form (*P. corneus*) is often seen in tropical aquaria, but care should be taken to exclude these snails from breeding tanks, because they will consume fish eggs. Ramshorn Snails are smaller than Apple Snails, with the Red species attaining a maximum size of about 1.25 cm (½ in).

Certain snails such as the Japanese Live-bearing Snail (*Viviparus malleatus*) are more suited to a cold water environment. This mollusc, as its name suggests, gives birth to live offspring, and will not damage plants in the aquarium. By contrast, *Limnaea* species can become pests in a planted tank, although it may be possible to overcome their destructive habits to some extent by adding supplementary food such as well-washed lettuce leaves, weighted down on the floor of the aquarium. *Limnaea* snails can be useful because they will remove *Hydra* from a tank.

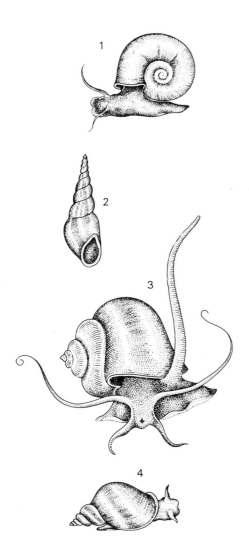

Four snails commonly seen in aquaria:
1 Ramshorn snail;
2 Malayan pond snail;
3 *Ampullaria* with proboscis extended;
4 *Limnaea*, can be destructive in a planted aquarium.

Maintaining aquarium equipment

Once the tank is established, its components must be checked closely each day. If there is no alarm system, the thermometer should be watched for any signs of fluctuation in water temperature, which may indicate a defect in the heating system. Damage can, in fact, be caused by the fish themselves, as certain larger species such as Oscars may attack heaters or thermostats for no apparent reason. If this does occur, it is safer to protect the heating apparatus in a suitably-sized glass jar, although circulation of the water may be impaired as a result. When there is any reason to suspect a fault, the power supply must be disconnected immediately, before anything else is done. Water in its impure state is an efficient conductor of electricity.

The pump will need to be serviced every three months or so, to remove accumulated debris which has been drawn in with the air. Tobacco smoke can be a particular problem, and may be introduced via the pump into the tank with disastrous consequences. Guppies can be killed in this way with very small quantities of smoke, and studies have shown that exposing females to smoke blown over the top of the tank causes sterility, and deformed fry in the case of pregnant guppies.

Problems with aeration in the tank may not result exclusively from a defective pump. The outlet tubing might have got blocked or accidentally kinked, which will reduce its efficiency, while air stones, too, can become blocked. Filter media must also be changed at regular intervals, every two or three weeks or so depending on the aquarium concerned.

Plant problems

If the plants do not appear to be thriving, then the amount of illumination which the tank is receiving may need to be increased. Those which feed through their roots, such as cryptocornes and *Echinodorus* may benefit from the occasional provision of a pellet of fertilizer. Some aquarists use a rabbit or guinea-pig dropping buried in the substrate nearby for this purpose. Alternatively a suitable tonic can be prepared using a proprietary plant food mixed thoroughly with clean clay, rolled into a pellet. A relatively common problem with *Echinodorus* and also *Vallisneria*, especially the Giant form, is that the leaves turn white, and then transparent with new growth appearing retarded. Ultimately the plants start to rot away. This disorder is known as chlorosis, and results from a specific lack of iron in their environment.

Amongst other problems, algal contamination of plant leaves can occur, especially in a tank with catfish which stir up the substrate. Careful wiping of the leaves will remove this unwelcome growth.

The plants in an aquarium will need thinning out occasionally, not only to give the fish more swimming room, but also to prevent their growth becoming stunted. Surface plants such as duckweed may have to be scraped off regularly if their growth becomes too luxuriant, to allow sufficient light to penetrate through to plants rooted at the bottom of the tank.

New introductions

There will be a time when new fish are to be introduced to the established tank. This must be undertaken cautiously to minimize the risk of introducing disease, and to protect the new arrivals from bullying. A small quarantine tank is essential, where these fish can be acclimatized to new surroundings and a check kept on their appetites and general health for about a fortnight before they are transferred to the main tank. A second tank set-up is also useful in an emergency against a failure in the main heating system, as the necessary component can be transferred immediately, assuming it has been cleaned after previous use.

Catching and handling fish

When fish have to be moved, they are usually caught by means of a net, although with very large fish, an anaesthetic may be added to their water to facilitate capture and to lessen the risk of injury. There are various designs of net available, the majority being made from nylon, although muslin is probably a softer option. Square or rectangular nets are suitable for use in the average tank, and these should be about 10 cm (4 in) in depth, obviously depending on the fish that has to be caught. Nets are quite cheap to purchase, and it is advisable to have a separate one for each tank, because disease can easily be transferred by this means.

Catching fish in a tank requires a degree of stealth, as well as patience. The net should be placed gently in the tank, and moved in the direction of the fish to be caught. It is often easier in a planted tank to catch fish at the front, where there are fewer obstructions, such as rocks or plants, which could snag the net. Once the fish is close to the net, a sudden upward movement of the net should serve to retain it. The free hand should be used to cover the mouth of the net once it is out of the water, to prevent the fish jumping out accidentally. Then with minimum delay, the fish can be transferred to its new environment. Fish should not be handled if possible, and only with wet hands when essential, to prevent damage to their sensitive skins. Some catfish are positively dangerous to handle, because of their poisonous spines. The common coldwater catfish, a member of the *Ictalurus* genus, is typical of this group and a prick from its spines can prove quite painful.

The rim of a net is relatively hard, and can injure fish, especially those with large fins. Binding tape around the rim will provide some padding, but there is an alternative safer method for catching such fish. A plastic bag is introduced to the tank and the fish to be caught is driven into the open mouth by a net or planting stick. This technique is probably also less traumatic than direct netting. The bag itself can be 'baited' with daphnia to attract the fish in by themselves if there is no urgency over catching them. Another method, which is very suitable for Spiny eels (*Macrognathus aculeatus*) as they will disappear into the substrate when threatened, requires a length of rubber tubing of suitable diameter. This is placed on the floor of the tank, and within a few hours, the eels will enter and hide in the piping, which is then removed with them *in situ*, thus causing minimum disturbance to the remainder of the aquarium.

Coping with power cuts

Power cuts present a potentially life-threatening situation for the occupants of a tropical aquarium, and under these conditions, it is vital to insulate the tank as much as possible. Thick expanded polystyrene cut to size and fixed around the outside of the tank with adhesive tape is very useful for this purpose, and can even be used on a daily basis to reduce heating costs. The hood should be left in place, and the top of the tank also covered with a quilt or thick blanket to restrict heat loss. It is safer to disconnect the apparatus from the mains supply, and then plug in again as soon as power is restored. Covering over the hood when the lights could come on unexpectedly presents an obvious fire risk.

There is no point in disturbing the coverings to note the water temperature, because this will lose vital heat. At room temperature, the water will cool down relatively slowly, enabling the fish to adjust to the change gradually. The reverse process occurs once the heating system is functioning again, and although not recommended, most tropical fish will survive a gradual fluctuation in the temperature of their surroundings. In a dire emergency, paraffin heaters can be used close to the tank, but apart from the risk of fire, the vapour given off will pollute the water unless the tank is adequately covered.

Holiday time

Fish present less of a difficulty at holiday time than other pets, although adequate preparation must be carried out in advance of departure. A partial water change is likely to be beneficial and all equipment, such as filters and pumps, should be overhauled as necessary. It is also important to check the electrical wiring.

Whilst the average fish can probably fast for two weeks or so without ill-effects, it is now possible to obtain both 'week-end' and 'vacation' food blocks. These are placed in the tank and offer a constant release of food to the fish over a given period of time without contaminating the water. If a friend or neighbour who has no experience of fish is persuaded to come in and check the tank daily, it is vital to stress the need not to overfeed its occupants. The provision of a spare heating system, and lighting, will ease the burden on the friendship should any apparatus malfunction during the holiday period.

Finally, remember to stress that if it is necessary to place a hand in the water, then the electrical equipment must always be switched off first as a precautionary measure.

4 Breeding

Breeding fish in an aquarium can add greatly to the enjoyment of keeping them. While certain species, like the guppy, are extremely free-breeding, there are others which present much more of a challenge for the determined aquarist. Details concerning the breeding requirements of particular fish are discussed in the second section of the book, whereas this chapter is concerned with general principles. It is well worth observing and making notes on the breeding behaviour of rarer species, which when combined with information on the feeding routine and water chemistry, may well add significantly to knowledge about their reproductive habits. Such articles when published in the specialist fish-keeping magazines are invariably of benefit to fellow aquarists. There is particular scope for those who wish to concentrate on a specific group of fish to highlight individual differences between the apparent needs of the various species. Serious breeding attempts will, however, necessitate more space for tanks, apart from increased expenditure on equipment.

Detecting breeding condition

There are various physical signs which indicate that a fish is entering breeding condition; females appear fatter, for example. Body coloration often becomes brighter at this time, and new colours may even appear, as in the case of the Three-spined Stickleback (*Gasterosteus aculeatus*) which develops a red belly. Most fishes when breeding become more active and may turn against other members of a community tank. Fatalities can occur at this stage, unless the fish are separated. If no spare tank is available, partitioning the aquarium using a suitable divider may be the only alternative.

Mode of reproduction

Female fish of some species reproduce by means of eggs whereas others give birth to live young. In the case of egg-layers, the male fertilizes the eggs once they have been laid, being in close proximity to the female at this time. When live-bearers were first studied in

Male sticklebacks (*Gasterosteus aculeatus*) develop red bellies when in breeding condition.

aquaria, it was assumed that males did not actually copulate with their mates, but released their semen nearby, and this was drawn into the female's body via the genital opening. Work with platies confirmed, however, that actual physical contact took place, but lasted only for a fraction of a minute. After a single mating, females of the family Poeciliidae can have a number of broods without further contact with a male fish. Paul Hahnel, who helped to establish the popularity of the guppy, recorded the production of seven consecutive broods as the result of a single mating in this species.

Nesting behaviour is not uncommon with fish which are breeding. The stickleback (*Gasterosteus* species) is a typical example, while various anabantid fish construct so-called 'bubble nests' at the water's surface. These are comprised of air trapped in mucus, giving rise to the bubble, and plants are also often included, serving to anchor the structure in place. Some killifish bury their eggs in the bottom of the shallow pools where they live until the pools dry up. When the next rains come, these eggs protected in the mud then hatch, giving rise to the next generation of killifish. As would be expected, these fish reach maturity quickly, by the age of three months whereas others, such as Blackline Tetras (*Hyphessobrycon scholzei*), will not usually breed before six months of age.

Another fish whose eggs survive out of water is *Copeina arnoldii*. In this case, both fish leap out of the water simultaneously, and the female lays her eggs on an overhanging leaf where they are fertilized by the male. Once back in the water the male remains in the vicinity of the eggs above, soaking them regularly by splashing at the water surface with his tail.

A pair of discus. These fish stay in close proximity to each other.

Left *Haplochromis burtoni* – a mouth-brooding cichlid.

1

The pairing off of fish is not usually a permanent phenomenon; a lasting bond is rarely formed. The signs of bonding in the case of discus (*Symphysodon discus*) are a pair remaining close together, nudging each other and repelling other fish which approach them. Not all fish will accept their intended mates, however, and when Oscars (*Astronotus ocellatus*) are seen snapping at each other's jaws, this is a sign that they will not form a satisfactory pair, and if left together, one may be injured as a result. Indeed, a few cichlids can be rather selective over their choice of mate, and some members of the genus *Channa* may restrict themselves to just one single partner.

Any form of parental care for eggs or offspring is rare in the case of fish, although there are exceptions. Some members of the *Tilapia* and *Haplochromis* genera for example, do not deposit their eggs, but retain them in their mouths until they hatch, and then care for the fry in a similar manner. The female normally carries out this task, but it is not unknown for the male to assist her. When breeding, therefore, these fish do not feed for at least three weeks.

Some adult fish are adapted to nourish their offspring. Young discus nibble for a period on the skins of their parents while some species of *Mystus* catfish actually produce a milky secretion which is rich in protein for their offspring. The young fish attach to their parents and obtain nourishment clinging on by their teeth to a primitive nipple, located on the undersurface of the adults.

In spite of these isolated instances of parental care, the majority of young fry face a very hazardous existence, and may often fall prey to members of their own species. Eggs are even more vulnerable to predation and so the number produced by egg-laying species is large, usually running into hundreds, and out of these, only a handful of fish will naturally survive to maturity. In species such as the sticklebacks, relatively fewer eggs are laid by the females, but these are protected in a nest rather than scattered randomly in the water. Fish eggs generally tend to sink, and are adhesive by nature, so that they often stick on to plants in the vicinity where they were

2

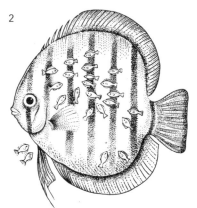

3

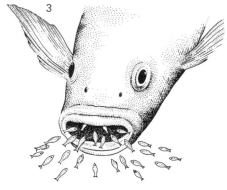

Brood protection in cichlids:
Top   substrate spawner (*Cichlasoma meeki*), with young;
Centre young discus fish feeding on the parent's flank;
Above mouthbrooder (*Tilapia*) with young retreating into the parent's mouth.

Mystus catfish may nourish their offspring. *Mystus vittatus* from south-east Asia is shown here.

laid. Vegetation serves to camouflage and protect the eggs until they hatch, which can be a matter of days, or even months later in the case of killifish. Most eggs hatch within a fortnight of being laid, although this will be influenced by the temperature of the water.

In the case of live-bearing species, there is less risk of losses amongst the next generation and consequently fewer fry are produced. This mode of reproduction helps to overcome the critical period when many of the eggs of oviparous species are destroyed. Unlike mammals, however, where the placenta forms a vital link between mother and offspring, there is no such connection in live-bearing fish, and the female's body simply acts as a safe refuge for the eggs until they are ready to hatch. Such species often produce less than 100 fry, which emerge bent in half but soon straighten out. The female carries her brood for a relatively long period, ranging between three weeks and three months in most cases, with the temperature of the water influencing the duration of gestation.

Unfortunately, as with egg-layers, it is not always possible to breed live-bearers successfully in a community tank, because the fry are often eaten. Pregnant females are kept isolated to maximize the number of offspring which are reared. If this system is adopted, females should be moved relatively early because they can be upset by rough handling and their brood is likely to be aborted before the young fish are able to survive independently outside their mother's body.

Conditioning fish to breed

In the wild state, breeding is stimulated by a change in the environmental surroundings of the fish, and this can be mimicked to some extent in aquaria. A varied diet, with an increased level of protein, is recommended for conditioning, together with livefood, which encourages activity. If possible, the sexes should be separated for three weeks before being re-introduced. A small increase in the temperature of their water can prove of benefit, while more lighting proves a stimulus with coldwater fish, which are normally exposed to seasonal changes. The condition of the water is significant and introducing a pair to a fresh tank may produce success. With fish which prove reluctant to breed, it has been possible experimentally to inject them with specific hormones to stimulate reproductive activity, but such techniques are not available to the average aquarist.

The set-up of breeding aquaria is rather dependent on the species concerned. With certain egg-layers, such as angelfish, which persist in laying their eggs on the heater, where they are destroyed, the only alternative is to place the heater in a protective covering comprised of a suitable glass jar. Bubble-nest builders must be kept in covered aquaria to prevent draughts destroying their nests. Other specific requirements are discussed later.

Bubble-nest builders, such as the Fighting Fish (*Betta splendens*) seen here below their nest, need to be kept in covered aquaria.

Care of the fry

The young of egg-laying species tend to be smaller than those of live-bearing fish. There is a considerable discrepancy in their size, however, ranging from cichlids which are quite large on hatching, down to the tiny anabantids. Size alone does not give an indication of the difficulty in rearing them, because some small fry have relatively large mouths and so are easier to cater for successfully. The young fish are dependent on the reserves of food present in their yolk sacs until these are exhausted, and during this period they remain inactive, hiding away in vegetation and other suitable sites. Breeding traps for live-bearers are favoured by some aquarists to protect the brood. The female herself remains confined in the trap while the fry can escape through the sides into the remainder of the tank, which enables them to avoid their potentially rapacious mother.

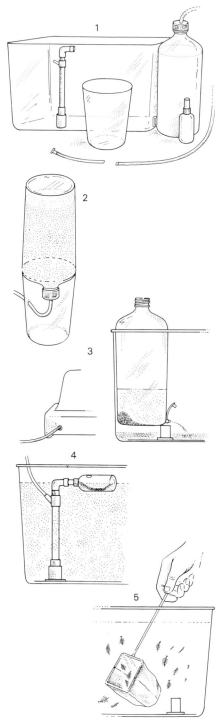

The hatching and rearing of brine shrimps (*Artemia*):
1 the general equipment required;
2 hatching the larvae from the eggs;
3 transferring larvae to the rearing tank;
4 introducing food for the larvae;
5 removing adult brine shrimps for feeding to the fish.

Young fish need to be kept in a relatively small aquarium, where suitable food is nearby. If they are not in close proximity to food, they are very likely to starve. Since fry are unable to consume large amounts of food at one sitting, they need to be fed small amounts perhaps five times during the day. Gentle aeration may be useful, but not for aquaria containing bubble-nest builders.

Food for fry

In the case of small-mouthed fry, they will require infusoria or a commercially-prepared substitute. Infusoria is a collection of minute microscopic organisms which develop in water containing vegetable matter. It is easily prepared by leaving crushed lettuce leaves, banana skins or even turnip slices in a jar of dechlorinated water for several days. Hay can also be used as an alternative, but must first be treated with boiling water, which serves to break down the cell walls. As the culture develops, the water will turn pinkish and cloudy, indicating the development of the protozoa, and then clear. Small volumes can be introduced via a pipette or spoon to the tank containing the fry. Unfortunately the protozoa *Paramecium* will not survive well in heated water, and so must be given in limited quantities. Infusorians are especially useful for newly-hatched anabantids. As a guide, 100 fry will empty a 1 kg (2.2 lb) jam jar of infusoria daily.

Brine shrimps (*Artemia*) are good rearing food for slightly larger fry. They are purchased from aquatic dealers in the form of eggs, which must be hatched in saltwater. Various methods are recommended for hatching these small crustaceans, and commercial kits are available, but the results obtained are not always successful. The technique outlined here was devised at the University of Ghent in Belgium, and proved itself in the rearing of a large number of young seahorses (*Hippocampus histrix*). It has several advantages over more commonly used methods, although it is slightly more laborious.

The first step is to add the eggs to dechlorinated water, allowing a maximum of 4 g of eggs per 100 cc of water. The water must then be well aerated for about an hour, so that the thick outer covering around the eggs is thoroughly permeated by water. An equal volume of 5 per cent sodium hypochlorite is then added, and the solution aerated for a further twenty-five minutes. This treatment serves to destroy the hard indigestible shell surrounding the eggs, leaving behind the immature shrimps protected in a membrane.

The shrimps which are then pinkish-orange in colour must be washed thoroughly under a running tap until no trace of the smell of the hypochlorite remains. They should be transferred finally to a suitable container such as a clean milk bottle containing a solution comprised of 30 g (1 oz) of sodium chloride dissolved in 1 litre

(1¾ pt) of dechlorinated tap water. Given adequate aeration and kept at a temperature of 25°C (77°F), the nauplii, which are the larval form of the brine shrimp, will hatch within about twelve hours or so, which is approximately half the time of more conventional methods. They can then be sieved and offered to the fry.

There is no need to worry about separating the indigestible shells from the nauplii using this technique, because all the shells are removed by chemical means. If inadvertently consumed by the fry, these shells can block their intestines, and also pollute the water. Eggs which fail to hatch are not wasted, as they can be consumed without their shells. Indeed, it is now possible, and simpler, to acquire brine shrimp eggs commercially in this form.

Setting up several cultures in succession will ensure a constant supply of the shrimps, although it is a false economy to purchase a relatively large quantity of brine shrimp eggs, because they are likely to deteriorate. Once a pack is opened, those which are not being used must be kept in an air-tight container, such as a screw-top jar. The jar itself must be completely dry, because the eggs take up moisture readily, and this seriously affects their hatchability. They must also be kept cool, in a temperature below 29°C (85°F).

In the case of the smallest fry, which cannot cope with brine shrimps on hatching, these can be introduced gradually from the age of about six days onwards. Other suitable foods include tiny microworms, while an inert item which is a reliable stand-by, especially in an emergency, is hard-boiled egg yolk. Fine particles can be separated using the sieves recommended previously for daphnia, or by means of muslin so that there is no risk of the fry choking on large particles. Egg-yolk must only be fed in restricted amounts, because any excess will tend to cloud the water.

Genetics and mutations

Mutations in fish arise as in other animals when the genes responsible for a particular characteristic such as colour, are modified. All genes occur on paired structures known as chromosomes, and fish have, in fact, been used as genetic models for the study of chromosomal abnormalities in humans. In the case of the normal male, the pair of chromosomes determining the individual's sex are of differing length, and thus distinguishable from all other pairs. This pair is referred to as XY, with Y being the shorter member of the pair.

Dr Hamilton, working at the Downstate Medical School, Brooklyn, New York, selected killifish to further studies into trisomy in humans. He dosed males with high levels of female sex hormones, to turn them into breeding females. From these fish, a proportion of the offspring were YY, mimicking the condition where a proportion of males have an extra Y chromosome. When introduced alongside normal female and male killifish, these YY individuals

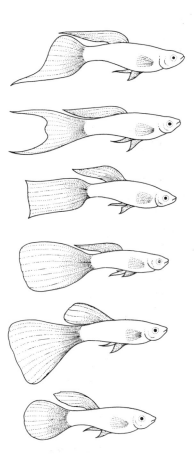

Standard forms of Guppy:
bottom sword
double sword
flagtail
veiltail
fantail
round tail

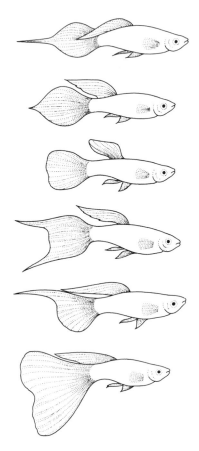

Standard forms of
Guppy (cont.):
pintail
speartail
spadetail
lyretail
top sword
triangle

proved more aggressive, but lived for a shorter period. The results appeared to correlate with observations on human patients suffering from this genetic abnormality and fuelled speculation that Y chromosomes do have a role to play in determining the individual's lifespan.

Chromosomes are also vital when cross-breeding of species is attempted. Hybridization depends on the individuals concerned possessing the same number of chromosomes. The guppy, for example, possesses forty-six, whereas Siamese Fighting Fish only have forty-two, so it is impossible for these fish to breed together successfully. Hybridization may occur between some members of the community tank. Swordtails (*Xiphophorus hellesi*) have been crossed with platies (*X. maculatus*) giving rise to a wide range of attractively-coloured hybrids.

When mutant or hybrid forms first occur, it takes careful husbandry to maintain them successfully. Such stock is often weak, with the original strain of Golden Angelfishes, for example, being handicapped by sterility and blindness. The Dovetail form of guppy, first bred in New York, only produced very small numbers in each brood in the early days of its existence. Indeed, not all mutations are established, but remain elusive. Four Albino Fighting Fish were recorded over a thirty-year period up to 1969 in America but could never be bred in any numbers. Some mutants die out completely, as happened with the so-called Robson Guppy, named after the original breeder, which disappeared shortly after the accidental death of Mr Robson himself. He never revealed the origins of this supposed mutant, and some aquarists felt that it was in fact a hybrid.

Hi-fin Swordtail, showing its enlarged
dorsal fin.

Once established, difficulties may persist with a particular mutation. The male Hi-fin Swordtail, which has an enlarged dorsal fin, also often suffers from an abnormally large copulatory organ or gonopodium. This can be cut back, but frequently regrows, and artificial insemination of the females has been used successfully by some breeders to overcome the problem. The technique is facilitated by the use of an anaesthetic added to the water to immobilize the fish. The development of mutations remains controversial in some quarters, and whether such patent deformities as the enlarged gonopodium of the Hi-fin should be encouraged is a question for the individual's conscience.

5 Diseases

The majority of diseases that affect aquarium fish can be traced directly back to their environment. The chemical composition of their water has been discussed previously, and significant alterations are likely to have lethal consequences. Sudden changes in pH, for example, will cause convulsions and ultimately death, as essential bodily activities, such as heart contractions, cease, causing oxygen starvation in other organs, especially the brain. Having set up the aquarium correctly, regular checking of the pH, and partial water changes as suggested previously will eliminate this potential hazard to the fishes' health. Aquarium water tends to increase in alkalinity as a result of the various chemicals which enter solution over a period of time, so toxic levels of ammonia are correspondingly raised.

DH readings must also be taken regularly, especially in breeding tanks. If the overall hardness is low, it is not unusual for the fry of some species, such as the Glowlight Tetra (*Hemigrammus marginatus*), to succumb with constitutional dropsy before they are even free-swimming. The temperature of the water is another important factor, because as it rises, the amount of oxygen present in solution decreases. Fish suffering from an oxygen deficiency are seen gasping at the surface.

In the well-balanced tank, which is regularly maintained and not overcrowded, such problems are unlikely to be encountered. Strict hygienic precautions over the feeding of fresh livefoods and the introduction of new fish will serve to minimize the risk of disease affecting the tank's occupants. The advances made in feeding fish over the past few years have ensured that nutritional diseases are now rare although they can still occur. Guppies, for example, are prone to spinal curvature if their diet is deficient in vitamin C, while fish fed low levels of vitamin A can suffer from blindness, stunting and haemorrhage affecting the base of the fins. An excessive intake of fat may result in lipoid liver degeneration, so the liver is enlarged and covered in haemorrhages, causing the fish to appear anaemic. All possible fat should therefore be removed when preparing offal for fish food.

Bacterial diseases

Bacterial infections in fish are generally caused by members of the Gram-negative group, and out of these the most dangerous is piscine tuberculosis, which was first recognized in 1897 and is still quite prevalent. Losses can be very high during outbreaks of tuberculosis and the symptoms are quite variable, ranging from emaciation to exophthalmia, causing the eyes to protrude unnaturally. Body coloration may fade while damage to the scales and fins is also often noticeable. Fish affected with tuberculosis are generally lethargic and refuse to feed. Such symptoms are associated with other diseases, but a confirmatory diagnosis can be made in a laboratory. A veterinarian will advise on carrying out the necessary tests if an outbreak of tuberculosis is suspected in the aquarium.

Although humans cannot contract tuberculosis from affected fish, it is possible for skin complaints to develop following contact with contaminated water or the fish themselves. As a general precaution, rubber gloves should be worn when cleaning the tank. Treatment of fish suffering from tuberculosis is generally not successful, and the aquarium should be emptied and washed out with an iodine-based disinfectant in this case to kill the bacteria. Following a very thorough rinsing, it can then be re-used safely.

Dropsy This is not a disease in itself, but a description of a symptom. A swollen abdomen is the characteristic sign, but the actual causes may be infectious or non-infectious. *Aeromonas* bacteria can cause dropsy and lead to sudden losses, with fish going off their food. These bacteria are often isolated from cases in conjunction with a virus. Infectious dropsy is seen especially in goldfish, and although treatment rarely proves effective, the complaint itself does not generally assume epidemic proportions.

Skin diseases of bacterial origin Damage to the fins or gills will enable bacteria, as well as other pathogens such as various fungi, to gain a hold on the unfortunate fish. Some species are more prone to such complaints than others, with fin rot, for example, being commonly encountered in Black Mollies. These can be classed as 'opportunist infections' as no single bacteria is implicated in every case.

In the community tank, fin-nipping can have severe consequences. Certain fish, such as Zebra Danios (*Brachydanio rerio*), are notorious 'nippers' and should not be kept alongside species with long fins such as angelfish. It is not always easy to spot the culprit, because nipping may occur even when the light is switched off. Close observation will be necessary to spot the aggressor, while suspects may have to be moved to another tank for confirmation.

In order to prevent a bacterial infection developing at the site of a nipped or damaged fin, neutral acriflavine, or a proprietary remedy used for fin rot should be added to the water at the appropriate dilution. The water temperature can also be raised slightly to 25°C (77°F). Fins will regenerate quite effectively, although they often remain relatively dark in colour for a long period, until the cell pigments are re-organized.

When dealing with sick or injured fish, it is useful to have a separate hospital tank where they can recover, without having to compete with their companions for food. Treatments added to the main tank may also present problems. Constant exposure to neutral acriflavine over a period of time will decrease growth rate, and can lead to sterility and liver damage. It is said that the use of livefoods, especially daphnia, during the treatment helps to minimize these adverse reactions, but obviously exposing healthy fish to such chemicals is not recommended. If acriflavine is used, it is important that the neutral form, and not the acid preparation, is obtained.

Treatments Antibiotic treatments for bacterial infections of fish are now being used quite widely, but they are not effective against viruses and only a small proportion have proved useful in counteracting fungal diseases. Suitable antibiotics can be obtained in Britain only from veterinarians, but elsewhere, they are more widely available. While in larger fish it is possible with care to inject the drug directly, a soluble form of treatment is most commonly used in aquaria. This will usually colour the water, terramycin turning it yellow for example; but more significantly, the antibiotic is likely to destroy many of the beneficial bacteria present in the established tank. The effects can be severe especially where an undergravel filter is being used. Fish to be treated should therefore be transferred to another tank.

Other remedies can also damage the bacterial flora. Methylene blue falls in this category, and will, in addition, stain the silicone rubber sealant. Some chemicals used to treat fish ailments, such as malachite green, formalin and salt have a less harmful effect if used at the correct dilutions. Unfortunately, many proprietary remedies also will be partially inactivated by filtration over carbon, so that in a hospital tank, a basic poly-foam filter is recommended.

Viral infections

Various viruses affecting fish have been identified, and some of these are particularly significant for the fish farming industry. Spring viraemia in carp is a notifiable disease in this category, seen especially in the spring when water temperatures are rising. It results in haemorrhages around the mouth and gills, and can concern the aquarist because goldfish may also succumb to this virus. The swim-bladder is affected in some cases, typically in younger fish. The rhabdovirus concerned is often identified with *Aeromonas* bacteria, while the various conditions are grouped together as the carp-dropsy complex. There is no treatment for the virus.

Parasitic diseases

Diseases of this group are of particular significance to the aquarist, especially those caused by unicellular organisms known as protozoa. The most widespread disease in this category results from infection by *Ichthyophthirius multifiliis*, abbreviated to 'Ich' or 'Ick', which causes the condition known as white spot. The characteristic small white spots can develop all over the body, but they are only one stage in the life cycle of this parasite.

Actual multiplication of the parasite takes place off the fish. The spots fall off, and the resulting cysts can each give rise to up to 1000 tomites (the free-swimming stage). They must find a host within about twenty-four hours after hatching, depending on the temperatures of the water, if they are not to die. In an aquarium therefore, the introduction of just one fish suffering from this disease can lead to an epidemic, as the tomites have no difficulty in finding hosts. Overcrowding will make an outbreak of white spot even more serious.

The tomites burrow into the fish's skin, giving rise to the characteristic white spot. Here they cause irritation and skin damage, which predisposes to secondary infections by opportunist bacteria and fungi. Once the tomites have embedded to form the trophozoite stage, they are difficult to destroy. Sequential treatment aimed at eliminating all tomites before they can embed is therefore necessary. Various proprietary remedies are available from aquarist shops, and chemical treatment with formalin, often in conjunction with malachite green, is also effective.

The scale of the disease, and the resulting financial cost, which is estimated at one million dollars per annum in America alone, has encouraged research into possible means of actually preventing it. Early attempts to produce a vaccine were hampered by the difficulties encountered in maintaining the protozoa satisfactorily under laboratory conditions. Working with a closely related species, scientists at the University of Georgia College of Veterinary Medicine achieved a breakthrough, and were granted a patent to produce a vaccine during 1982. Although currently it has to be given by individual injection, it is hoped that the vaccine will be developed for mass administration, either via the feed or in the water. The benefits of this research will undoubtedly become more widely available to all those involved with fish over the course of the next few years.

Apart from 'Ich', there are various other protozoal diseases of concern to aquarists. *Oodinium pillularis* has a similar life-cycle to *Ichthyophthirius*, and like another dinoflagellate protozoa, *Amyloodinium*, causes Velvet Disease. *Amyloodinium* generally attacks only the gills, rather than the whole body. Young fish die quickly from Velvet Disease, with labyrinth fish and danios appearing most susceptible. It is not always easy to recognize the disease, but the presence of minute yellowish-brown marks on the body, with the fish rubbing itself against rocks to ease the irritation, are highly suggestive of this complaint.

Amongst other types of parasite, flukes attaching to the skin or gills may be encountered occasionally. Members of the Cyprinidae and Characidae families are most commonly afflicted with such flukes. Those which attack the gills are more serious, and harder to eliminate successfully, since their eggs often prove immune to treatment. Repeated therapy is necessary to destroy the young flukes once they have hatched. They cause irritation to the gill membranes, leading to excessive mucus production, which may well prove fatal. Flukes normally gain access to the aquarium either with the fish themselves or with contaminated livefood.

Internal parasites do not usually present severe problems for the aquarist, but various worms and trematodes may infect fish. Their life cycles can be quite complex, and involve other creatures such as snails. Signs of infection are fairly non-specific in most cases, although blindness is often indicative of the presence of trematode larvae damaging the lens of the eye. The fish is the intermediate host, as the adult form of the parasite is only seen in birds. Exophalmia (also known as 'pop-eye') may be a symptom, but this can result also from other causes, such as tuberculosis. There is no specific treatment recommended for the endoparasites in fish.

Fungal disease

Fungal spores can be isolated from fish tanks, but often cause disease only when the fish's skin is damaged in some way. There are many different fungi grouped together in the family Saprolegniacea, but treatment of all fungal infections is similar irrespective of the cause. Effective remedies are produced by the major aquatic companies, or malachite green as a 1 per cent solution can be used. Apart from treating affected individuals, it is important to try to identify the precipitating factor. Rough netting or handling may be responsible, or if the eyes are affected, this is often a sign that the ammonia levels are too high, and caused the damage initially. Fungal infections show as areas of whitish strands, which can develop to resemble cotton wool in severe cases, with the fish being typically lethargic. In some cases, fish eggs will also be infected with fungus, and must be treated accordingly.

Bumble Bee Gobies (*Brachygobias xanthozona*). Their eggs are prone to fungal infections.

Miscellaneous diseases

Tumours of various types are not unknown in fish, with goldfish, for example, being susceptible to fibromas. These are usually confined to the head, and show as small, firm lumps. They do not appear to cause the fish much discomfort, but can be removed by surgery. A much more serious skin tumour is the malignant melanoma, encountered in offspring resulting from guppies mated with swordtails. This particular tumour is thought to be of genetic origin.

Constipation is not a serious problem in aquarium fish, but can be seen occasionally. Affected individuals have a trail of droppings attached to their anal opening which they are unable to expel completely. The addition of livefood, such as daphnia, to their diet should cure the condition, and prevent it recurring. Fish red exclusively on dry diets are most susceptible to constipation.

Dealing with disease

When faced with a severe outbreak of disease, the fish concerned can be sent for examination to a laboratory. Contact with such institutions can be made through a local veterinarian, who may also be able to help directly. The current regulations concerning the despatch of diseased fish to a laboratory should be ascertained, and it is often helpful if details such as their housing conditions, diet and symptoms are enclosed. A sample of water from their tank is also often useful to a laboratory. If possible, it is preferable to arrange an appointment and call in person, because it is then possible to take living specimens which are affected, rather than corpses, and these may be of more use to the scientists for their research.

Proprietary remedies are a great help to the aquarist, and should cope adequately with most common problems that can be treated. When using any treatment, however, the accompanying instructions on the pack should be followed closely, because some remedies, especially those containing copper, are very likely to prove toxic if used in excess.

When faced with sudden mysterious deaths in a tank, poisoning must be considered, especially if a large number of fish are affected. Many of the chemicals in every day use around the home, such as aerosol sprays, can prove toxic to fish. The air-borne particles will settle on the water surface, especially if the tank is not covered, and they can, in fact, be carried on local air currents for a considerable length of time. The threat of chlorine, and copper from newly-installed piping, has already been mentioned previously, as has cigarette smoke.

PART II THE FISH

Approximately 20,000 different species of fish are recognized by ichthyologists, occurring in a wide range of habitats. The Blue Desert Fish (*Cyprinodon macularis*) is found in areas of water in the Nevada Desert of North America, where the temperature of their surroundings may reach 40°C (104°F). The Ice-Fish (*Chaenocephalus*) of the Antarctic seas, in contrast, has developed chemicals in its blood which prevent it freezing to death.

Fish are quite adaptable creatures, as shown by experiments using goldfish. They can spawn in temperatures between 12°C (55°F) and 21°C (70°F), and will adjust to live in waters with temperatures in excess of 38°C (100°F). By way of contrast, tropical species can live in relatively cold surroundings. The temperature of lakes in Kenya may fall as low as 5°C (40°F) for part of the year, and yet the *Tilapia* cichlids will survive adequately under these conditions, and start to breed when the temperature rises again. *Tilapia* cichlids are also living wild in England, occurring in a section of a canal fed by hot water from an adjoining glassworks in Merseyside. They were liberated there some years ago, and are now thriving in a water temperature of between 21°-26°C (70°-80°F) along with other tropical species such as Convict Cichlids (*Cichlasoma nigrofasciatum*) and various mollies.

Even between aquarists, there may be a slight discrepancy in the temperature at which they maintain a particular species. European fish-keepers generally keep fish at slightly lower temperatures than their British counterparts, but the figures given in the following section give an indication of the suitable range. Subsequent maintenance of a relatively constant temperature is of equal significance for the majority of fish.

Supply and movement of fish

Although many aquarium fish are bred commercially, a proportion are still caught in the wild. The supply of such fish is often seasonal, because of trapping conditions. Collection in the Amazon Basin, for example, takes place during the dry season, when the water level is low and the fish are more concentrated in particular localities. New species are still being discovered: over half the specimens captured by one expedition during the late 1970s from the Matto Grosso region of Brazil were previously unknown.

Fish are usually caught by means of nets, located around the roots of floating plants. Discus, cichlids and angelfish are easily netted in this way. They are then transferred to barrels on the natives' boats, and taken to an exporter, who sorts the fish on arrival. Orders are then made up for despatch, and the fish packed with oxygen and possibly a tranquillizer in their water, before being flown out to their eventual destinations. Movement of fish from one country to another may be regulated by both health and conservation controls, so advice should be sought from the relevant authorities in advance.

Classification

Many fish are still referred to by their scientific names alone. This is usually comprised of two words, for example, *Poecilia reticulata* in the case of the guppy. The term '*reticulata*' describes the species, with species being defined as individual populations which can breed together successfully, although under normal conditions such hybridization is unlikely to occur. *Poecilia* is the generic term, shared with other related species such as *Poecilia velifera*, the Sailfin Molly. Similar genera are then grouped together in families, such as Poeciliidae in this case. Classification is sometimes revised as new facts emerge about the fish concerned. Guppies were, in fact, formerly placed in another genus, *Lebista*, before their relationship with other members of the *Poecilia* was appreciated.

6 Coldwater Fish

Sticklebacks

Various members of the family Gasterosteidae are found throughout most of Europe, extending into Asia, and even Japan, as well as North America. These fish all possess characteristic spines, ranging in number from three to fifteen, depending on the species concerned, in front of their dorsal fins. The Three-spined (*Gasterosteus aculeatus*) and Ten-spined (*Pygosteus pungitius*) occur in both fresh and brackish waters whereas the American Four-spined Stickleback (*Apeltes quadracus*) is usually confined to brackish surroundings. These three species are most commonly seen in aquaria.

Sticklebacks have aroused considerable scientific interest, because of their unusual territorial nesting behaviour. The reddish belly acquired by males during the breeding season has been shown to act as a challenge to any nesting males at this time. Male sticklebacks alone are responsible for constructing the hollow nests where breeding takes place. They are made from any suitable material, such as leaves or twigs, which are joined together by a sticky mucus secretion. Once it is complete, the male forces a female into the interior where, after a few minutes, her eggs are released and fertilized. Other females are also coerced into the nesting site, but having laid, they simply leave the eggs, which may eventually number several hundred, in the male's care. He guards the nest determinedly, driving off any potential rivals, and appears to aerate the eggs occasionally by blowing water through the nest.

As aquarium occupants, sticklebacks are aggressive and should not be housed with other coldwater species such as goldfish, because they can inflict savage wounds with their spines. They require a tank about 60 cm (2 ft) in length, well-planted with vegetation made up of *Elodea*, *Vallisnaria* and *Sagittaria*, which do well under coldwater conditions. A temperature of about 18°C (65°F) is quite suitable for these fish, and indeed they should not be exposed to temperatures over 21°C (70°F). As might be expected, sticklebacks are naturally carnivorous in their feeding habits, and should be treated accordingly, with plenty of livefood, such as whiteworm, included in their diet.

Pumpkin-seed Sunfish (*Lepomis gibbosus*).

Low temperatures are necessary to bring sticklebacks into breeding condition, and during the winter, their water should be allowed to cool down to as low as 5°C (41°F). One male can be kept with three or four females in a tank, but these should be removed after they have spawned. The young fish will hatch four to seven days later, as the nest begins to disintegrate. Infusoria or fine grade egg yolk for the first couple of days are recommended, followed by brine shrimps and small daphnia, which is a favourite of all stickle-backs. Males protect their offspring for a short time after hatching. Young sticklebacks can grow to a size of about 5.25 cm (2½ in).

Sunfishes

The sunfishes of the family Centrarchidae are natives of North America, found especially in central and eastern areas. In aquaria, they are relatively easy to cater for, but being strictly carnivorous, they will not take at all readily to inanimate prepared foods, and must be given fresh livefoods. Sunfish require slightly acid water, with a pH value of about 5, and a temperature in the range 15°-20°C (59°-68°F), which can fall slightly lower in the winter.

Over fifteen species of sunfish are known, and they will hybridize naturally in the wild. One of the most common in aquaria is the Pumpkin-seed Sunfish (*Lepomis gibbosus*), which ranges south from the Great Lakes to Florida and Texas. It is named after the characteristic appearance of the blotches on its head, and can grow to 20 cm (8 in) in size. Pygmy Sunfishes (*Elassoma evergladei*) are dwarfs in comparison, rarely attaining 2.5 cm (1 in) in length. They also have different breeding habits from other members of the family, as the female Pygmy lays in a nest, rather than a depression created by the male fanning his fins over the substrate.

The male displays to the female, and they then move to the nesting site. The eggs are protected by the male until they hatch about three days later, and the fry remain under his care for a further week or so. They must be reared on suitable livefood such as brine shrimps and small daphnia from the outset. Sunfish need to be kept on their own, and even a pair may quarrel amongst themselves, so a planted environment is recommended. They are not easy to sex outside the breeding season, until the male becomes more colourful.

Goldfish

Having been domesticated for centuries, goldfish are now bred in a wide range of colours and shapes, with some forms being considered as grotesque by all but their most loyal supporters. A Chinese scientist, Shisan Chen, has estimated that no less than 126 distinct breeds of fancy goldfish have been bred from the original form. While the true goldfish can reach a size of 30 cm (1 ft), the fancy varieties are generally smaller.

Goldfish can be obtained in a range of colours, from black and reddish-golden to yellow and silver, with speckled forms also available. Young goldfish are dark green at first, bordering on black, before lightening to their characteristic golden hue. Fry kept in dark surroundings from birth are slower to obtain their colour than those living in well-lit aquaria. The fish's colour can also be altered by changes in the tissue under its scales. Where the cells are modified, their ability to reflect light is altered as a result. These are referred to as 'calico' or 'nacreous' fish.

The Shubunkin is a calico variety that otherwise resembles the normal goldfish, although its tail is more ornamental, and the lobes of the fins are slightly rounded. Its name is derived from the Japanese term, meaning 'Vermilion Variegated Goldfish', which describes the variegated appearance of these fish. All calico fish are variegated, with those showing shades of blue considered most valuable. Another hardy, basic variety is the Comet, characterized by its enlarged, pointed tail and fins. Comets are bred in both normal and calico forms, although the latter variety are no longer exhibited. Normal Comets are usually deep red, but a yellow fish has been bred.

Fantails, as their name suggests, have an elaborate divided tail, as well as additional anal fins. Their bodies are less streamlined than the normal goldfish, being rounder in shape. Both scale types are recognized. Veiltails bred from Fantails have an even more elaborate caudal fin, causing it to hang in folds. They appear very graceful in an aquarium, but care should be taken to ensure that there are no rough edges on rocks, for example, where they could damage their trailing tails.

Veiltail Goldfish. Males of all varieties develop small white pimples on their gill plates, which are apparent only during the breeding period. These should not be confused with white spot (see page 59).

A variety resembling the two previous forms in the arrangement of its tail fins, but instantly distinguishable because of its jet black coloration, is the Moor. There is no calico form in this case. It is not easy to maintain the black appearance of Moors, however, because older fish of this type turn bronze rather than remaining black.

Moors can have protuberant eyes, and are then referred to as being 'telescope-eyed'. The eyes are usually positioned as for normal fish, but occasionally may point forwards. Various types of telescope eye are recognized by the enthusiast, and described accordingly, such as the 'segmented sphere' form. Protuberant eyes are not, in fact, evident in the fry, but usually develop when they are several months old. Fish with such eyes are virtually blind, but can detect their food without difficulty by means of scent.

One of the most distinctive goldfish mutants has been ascribed the exotic name of 'Lionhead', although the German description of 'Tomatohead' is perhaps more fitting. The heads of these fish are enlarged, and have an appearance which resembles a mass of wart-like growths. This distortion of the head reduces the flexibility of the gill plates, so Lionheads require well-aerated water to enable them to breathe without difficulty. The temperature of their water must not rise above 20°C (68°F) because otherwise the amount of oxygen in solution will be significantly reduced, causing them breathing distress.

Orandas have a similar appearance to Lionheads, and probably resulted from crossings of this latter variety with Veiltails. They possess dorsal fins, unlike Lionheads, but require similar careful management. The excrescences occur more on the top of the head, rather than the sides as in the case of the Lionhead. These growths can take four years to develop to their full extent.

There are various other types of ornamental goldfish which may be seen occasionally. Celestials, called 'Stargazers' by the Chinese, have their eyes positioned horizontally in their heads, so they look directly upwards. Pompons have resulted from an enlargement of the nasal septum, which partitions the nostrils. Egg-fish, first introduced to Britain from Japan in 1939, are named after the characteristic shape of their bodies. They lack dorsal fins. Some goldfish varieties are localized, with the Pearl Scale having originated in the Chinese province of Kwangtung. One of the newer varieties seen in the West called the Panda, is black and white.

Care of goldfish All goldfish will thrive in an aquarium where the water temperature is maintained at about 15°C (59°F). They are active by nature, and thus require adequate swimming space, so their tank must not be cluttered with rockwork. Their movement tends to keep debris in suspension, and thus a box-type filter is recommended to keep the tank clean. Fine-leaved plants such as *Myriophyllum* will soon have their leaves covered with mulm and may well be eaten by the goldfish. *Sagittaria* and *Vallisnaria* are better alternatives. Goldfish will eat a wide variety of foodstuffs, and are not difficult to cater for, using prepared foods as a basis for their diet, augmented by suitable livefoods.

Breeding Goldfish in their second year are preferable for breeding purposes. They are not easy fish to sex, although when in breeding condition the female swells with roe and appears fatter. They can lay as many as 500 eggs in batches, which hatch in four or five days, depending on temperature. The parents should be removed after spawning, because they will often eat the eggs. Infusoria should be provided at first for the young fry. A reservoir to ensure a constant supply of such food throughout the day can be easily established using a clean rubber tube and funnel. The tube itself is tied in position as necessary, and clamped sufficiently to allow only a drop or so of the infusoria contained in the funnel into the tank at regular intervals. Some cannibalism may occur amongst the young fish if there is much difference in their growth rates, and only fish of similar size should be kept together in a nursery tank, taking care to avoid overcrowding them.

White Cloud Mountain Minnows

Another Chinese species, these fish were discovered in the White Cloud Mountains near Canton by a scout called Tan, and they are also known, not surprisingly, as Tan's Fish. White Cloud Mountain Minnows (*Tanichthys albonubes*) require a water temperature preferably in the range 16°-20°C (61°-68°F) and must be kept in fresh water. They will give an early indication of a deterioration in the water's quality by gulping at the surface, and showing signs of loss of balance.

Mountain Minnows are relatively small, being about 5 cm (2 in) in length, and are brownish-green in colour, although this fades in older specimens. Females are smaller, and have pale red lips. In a well-planted tank, they show to good effect when kept in shoals. Individual pairs can be induced to spawn by raising the water temperature to about 22°C (72°F), and providing fine-leaved plants such as *Myriophyllum*. The female does not lay a vast number of eggs, rarely more than 200, but cannibalism is unlikely to be a problem if sufficient livefood is provided. The fry are swimming freely about a week after the eggs are laid, and will breed from the age of six months onwards.

7 Live-bearing Tropical Fish

The live-bearing tooth carps, which include guppies, swordtails and platies, are amongst the most suitable fish for the novice aquarist. The guppy (*Poecilia reticulata*) is ideal, because it will adapt and breed freely under a variety of conditions. Like other members of the family, these fish are easy to sex, with males possessing brightly coloured caudal fins. The female guppy, by contrast, is relatively dull and bigger than her mate. The size of the female is a significant feature when selecting breeding stock, because bigger females have proportionately larger broods. This phenomenon was fully investigated by Dr Affleck who published the following formula based on his studies: number of fry produced $= 5.2L - 15.5 - (0.7L - 14)$. 'L' in this case corresponds to the female's total length at the time of giving birth. He also devised a special breeding trap to prevent any cannibalism, which would have ruined his results.

Although guppies will live in temperatures as low as 15°C (64°F), they do best when kept in a temperature range of 25°-27°C (77°-81°F), with a near neutral pH and slightly hard water conditions, as for other live-bearers. At a temperature of 25°C (77°F), their gestation period is twenty-eight days. Keeping them at 32°C (92°F) reduces this time down to nineteen days, but also shortens the lives of the females. Guppies can breed successfully in a community tank, but it must be densely planted if the fry are to survive. Adults are not fussy about food, and will eat a variety of prepared and fresh livefoods, as well as vegetation, while their fry can be reared successfully on brine shrimps.

A wide range of fancy mutations are now established, with modifications to both the fins and colour of these popular fish. In order to preserve these new forms, pairing of closely-related fish is often necessary, and some of these newer, fancy varieties are more demanding in their requirements than the natural guppy. Colour-feeding can often benefit their appearance, particularly those fish with red markings. Before scientific formulations were available, aquarists used boiled carrots to achieve a good depth of coloration in their fish. The carrots were boiled in a minimum of water, and then chopped very finely and mixed into a paste with Bemax.

Guppies are prone to fluke infestations, with dropsy generally

Poecilia reticulata

being the first sign. Small swellings then develop on the body, and when these are carefully incised, the yellow immature stage of the fluke *Clinostomum marginatum* will be visible. These must be removed with tweezers, and Friar's Balsam, applied on cotton-wool buds, can be used to dress the wound. Several such treatments may be necessary before the wound heals. Guppies are also prone to body tilt, lying at an abnormal angle in the water. This could indicate a swim-bladder disorder, but occurs mainly in older fish and is regarded primarily as a symptom of senility, for which there is no treatment.

Mollies

Mollies occur naturally in North America, around the Gulf of Mexico, and are usually found in brackish conditions. Salt, about one teaspoonful to 4.5 litres (1 gal), should therefore be added to their aquarium water. Some species can grow quite large, reaching 15 cm (6 in) in length, and thus require adequate space. Mollies are primarily herbivorous in their feeding habits, and will browse contentedly on the resulting algae if their tank is kept in well-lit surroundings. Boiled lettuce and spinach can be offered as alternatives, or until the algae are established in the tank. Some livefood and dried matter will also be eaten by mollies.

There is one disease to which mollies seem especially prone. It is often referred to as 'mouth fungus', but this is incorrect as the infection is caused by a bacterium, typically *Chondrococcus columnaris* or a related species. Treatment using 100 mg of terramycin per 4.5 litres (1 gal) of water, can be successful.

One of the most common mollies seen in aquaria is the Black form. This is not, in fact, a particular species, but a hybrid strain developed from black individuals of other species. A similar form, known as the Lyretail Molly also has a hybrid ancestry, and was first bred in south-east Asia. Mollies require a water temperature between 23° and 28°C (74°-82°F), and because of their liking for vegetation, only relatively hardy plants, such as *Vallisneria*, should be included in their tank. Females are larger than males, which can be recognized by the presence of their copulatory organ or gonopodium.

Sailfin Mollies (*P. latipinna*) possess enlarged dorsal fins. Another closely related form is *P. velifera*. These fish must have an adequate swimming area to develop their enlarge tails. Various domesticated strains of the wild forms are now established, and one of the most attractive is the Black Velifera or Midnight Molly, which has yellowish-orange edging to its dorsal fin. The body coloration of this Sailfin is black, as its name suggests. Mollies normally have about eighty offspring, after a gestation period that can be as long as ten weeks.

Albino Sailfin Molly (*Poecilia velifera*).

Swordtails

The Swordtail (*Xiphophorus helleri*) is so-named after the characteristic caudal fin structure of the male. The lower rays are elongated into a sword-like shape. All members of this genus, which includes the platies, are confined to Mexico and Guatemala in Central America. The wild form of the swordtail is green, but selective breeding and hybridization have given rise to a wide range of colours, with red becoming especially prominent.

These fish make most attractive aquarium occupants, especially when kept in groups (or 'schools'), and although males sometimes squabble amongst themselves, they will not harm other fish. A tank for swordtails should be heated to between 22° and 25°C (72°-77°F), and planted around the back and sides, leaving adequate space for swimming in the front. They prefer medium-hard water, and will thrive on a varied diet that includes some livefood.

Breeding does not present any particular problem. As in other members of the family Poeciliidae, when the female is about to deliver her brood, the 'gravid spot' becomes visible near the vent. The spot itself is part of the peritoneum, and once visible, you cannot move the female without a serious risk of damaging her brood. If she has been transferred to a breeding trap beforehand, great care should be taken to ensure that it does not become fouled by excess feeding. Live daphnia is probably the best food for fish in such traps, but if dried foods are used, they should be given more or less as individual flakes, several times a day to satisfy her appetite.

An alternative is to set up a breeding tank, and then remove the female once she has released her brood. Swordtails may produce over 150 fry at a time, but these will often fall prey to any adults in their vicinity, unless there is adequate cover available in the form of fine-leaved plants. For breeding purposes, only one male is necessary for several females.

The swordtail (*Xiphophorus helleri*), like the guppy, has been bred in a number of forms.

The wide range of colours now being bred makes the wild swordtail seem a rather insignificant fish. While some of these are described simply in terms of colour, such as the Red or Golden, others are named after places which contributed to their development, such as the London, Wiesbaden and Berlin Swordtails. The 'green' type referred to by some aquarists is really a refined form of the wild swordtail.

Platies

Platies are very similar in their requirements to swordtails, and are now included in the same genus, although previously they were classified as *Platypoecilus* species, which gave rise to their common name. Two distinct forms, *Xiphophorus maculatus* and *X. variatus* are recognized, with the latter type sometimes being known as the Variegated Platy, although they will hybridize quite readily, and various colours are now firmly established. Hybrids produced between platies and swordtails are also fertile. Among the various platies recognized by aquarist societies are Red, Yellow, Black, Blue, Spangled, Leopard, Wagtail, Moon and Sunset forms. Gnat larvae are a popular livefood with these fish, which can be fed as for swordtails.

Other live-bearers

There are various other members of the family Poeciliidae which may be seen occasionally, including those belonging to the genus *Gambusia*. These fish are not recommended for the community aquarium, because they are inveterate fin-nippers and prove rather aggressive. They have, however, proved useful in controlling mosquito larvae in areas where malaria is endemic, as they will consume their body weight of these insects daily. The smallest known live-bearer is *Heterandria formosa*, sometimes referred to as the Mosquito Fish, which reaches barely 2.5 cm (1 in) in length. These fish are often bullied by large inhabitants of mixed tanks, and may even be eaten in some cases. Females produce several young daily over the course of a fortnight, and can have a brood every four weeks or so.

Apart from the live-bearing tooth carps, some other fish also give birth to young directly. These include members of the family Hemirhamphidae, commonly known as half-beaks, because of the unusual arrangement of their jaws. The lower mandible is elongated and immobile, while the upper one is much shorter. Several species are occasionally available, with *Dermogenys pusillus* being most common. These fish occur in South-east Asia, and are found in both fresh and brackish waters, and even out to sea in some cases. Males can be recognized by the presence of red on their

Dermogenys siamensis – a species of Half-beak.

dorsal fins, whereas females are larger, being approximately 8.75 cm (3½ in) in length.

Half-beaks live close to the water surface, and a temperature of 23°C (73°F) suits them well. When first acquired, they are often very nervous, and must be treated with caution. Their prominent lower jaw is easily damaged, which can prove fatal, and although regeneration may take place in less severe cases, it is rarely ever complete. A tank for half-beaks should have a good surface area, and contain floating plants for cover. They feed largely on insects captured near the surface, and so fruit flies are especially valuable for them as a source of food. Gnat larvae, daphnia and tubifex in a feeder are other possible alternatives. Food must be available at the surface, because half-beaks will not scavenge near the bottom of the tank.

When breeding, females should be transferred to a shallow tank containing about 15 cm (6 in) of water. They produce between fifteen and forty fry as a rule, which will take fruit flies and brine shrimps from an early age. The gestation period itself can be as long as two months, and it is not uncommon for the female to abort her young during this time. The young fish prefer a higher temperature than the adults, in the region of 28°C (82°F). Although half-beaks are not perhaps recommended for the novice, they present a challenge for the determined breeder, and make unusual tank occupants.

8 Egg-laying Tropical Fish

As a general rule, egg-layers are harder to breed successfully than their live-bearing counterparts, and a separate breeding tank is necessary to ensure satisfactory results. Once the eggs have been fertilized, adults which show no parental care should then be returned to the community tank. Failure to do this will result in the loss of a large number of eggs in many cases. Fish are only transferred a couple of days or so before spawning is expected, and so are not always fed over this brief period, in order to keep the water as clean as possible for the fry.

Egg-laying tooth carps

Egg-laying tooth carps, also referred to as killifish, are more suitable for the specialist aquarist, and are best kept in individual groups comprised of one species only. Over 500 different types are recognized, some of which have a seasonal life cycle, living in ponds which dry up for part of the year. They require soft water conditions, and some aquarists collect clean rainwater for their tanks. In certain areas, however, because of industrial pollution, rainwater contains dissolved nitric and sulphuric acid, and so its pH value may be too low. Although some killifish prefer acid conditions, others should be kept in neutral water.

These fish have a very wide distribution, and their breeding requirements are quite variable. Eggs may be laid on plants, while other species burrow in the substrate to prepare a suitable site. The fry may take weeks, months or even years in some cases to hatch, often being naturally stimulated by rainfall. It is possible to buy eggs and hatch them, rather than purchasing fish directly.

Members of the genus *Aplocheilus*, such as the Blue Panchax (*A. panchax*) live at the surface of the water, and should be kept in a tank with floating plants, such as *Ricca*. These killifish require livefoods, such as tubifex and fruit flies to form the major part of their diet, although they also accept some dried food. Amongst the most colourful species are those classified in the genus *Aphyosemion*, which occur in parts of Africa. The Lyretail (*A. australe*) is frequently seen, and requires a water temperature of about 22°C (72°F), with soft, acid conditions. *Epiplatys* species lay on plants.

Distribution of toothcarps.

Aplocheilus lineatus, with the male above.

Blue Panchax (*Aplocheilus panchax*).

Lyretail (*Aphyosemion australe australe*),
with female in the centre.

Aphyosemion gardneri.

Left *Epiplatys longiventralis*. A West African species, growing to about 6 cm (2¼ in).

Below *Nothobranchius rachovii*.

Above *Cyprinodon macularius,* male below.

Right Typical habitat of *Cyprinodon macularius,* at Saratoga Springs, USA.

and can be considered for a mixed tank. Males are bigger and more colourful than females.

The *Nothobranchius* killifish occur in eastern coastal regions of Africa, and reach a maximum size of about 6.25 cm (2½ in). They are bottom-spawners and will lay on a peat medium which should be provided as the substrate for their tanks. Fruit flies and other livefood like daphnia will prove acceptable to these fish. The easiest species to maintain are *N. orthonotus* and *N. palmquisti,* requiring a temperature between 22° and 24°C (72°-75°F), and water which is both acid (pH 6.8) and soft (6-10°DH). *N. rachovii* is slightly more delicate, needing softer and more acid water (2-5°DH: pH 6.5).

Amongst the American killifish, those belonging to the genus *Cyprinodon* occur in the desert areas of the United States, in the south-west of the country. They need hard brackish water (15-25°DH), and a temperature of 25°-27°C (77°-81°F). These species, and those of the South American *Pterolebias* genus lay in the substrate of their tanks, which should be aquarium peat, about 3.75 cm (1½ in) in depth. Male *Pterolebias* can become very aggressive when breeding. Softer water conditions (with a DH of less than 10°), and a lower temperature of 22°C (72°F), with an acid pH, will suit these killifish well.

Barbs and related species

There are approximately 1500 members in the family Cyprinidae, many of which are popular aquarium occupants. Although the goldfish is best-known out of the group, species in the genera *Barbus, Danio* and *Rasbora* are often represented in tropical tanks. The family as a whole is characterized predominantly by the absence of an adipose fin, and the development of barbels in many

Typical barb habitat in south-east Asia.

Distribution of the carp and barb family
(Cyprinidae).

Rosy Barb (*Barbus conchonius*).

cases. These have a sensory function, helping the fish to locate food around the substrate of their environment.

The tropical barbs are confined to south-east Asia and Africa, with no representatives of the group in America. They usually occur in shoals, and should be kept in groups in aquaria. Barbs are not difficult to maintain, requiring a water temperature in the region of 24°-25°C (25°-77°F) and relatively hard water conditions. Cryptocornes are ideal for planting in a tank to house barbs. These fish will accept a varied diet, although their lively natures are most apparent when they are offered livefood. Water in the tank must be well-aerated, because in the wild, most barbs occur in flowing rather than still water.

Members of the genus *Barbus* can be bred under aquarium conditions, and are not costly to purchase in the first instance. A large number are regularly available, and out of these, the Rosy Barb (*B. conchonius*) is one of the most attractive, with the breeding male assuming a bright red coloration, offset with a black spot on each side of the body towards the tail. The scales, which are a prominent feature of many barbs, are especially noticeable in this species. They require clean, clear water conditions, being found naturally in areas of running water in the eastern regions of India.

Breeding condition can be stimulated by increasing the amount of livefood in their diet. Rosy barbs are one of the easier species to breed successfully. They require a tank furnished with plenty of vegetation in thick clumps, and two males to one female can give better results. They will eat the eggs readily after spawning, and so must be removed as soon as possible. A covering of glass marbles over the floor of the tank will help to protect the eggs, which can slip down between them. The fry require infusoria or a commercial substitute on hatching, and later can be introduced to brine shrimps.

The two species of Tiger Barb (*B. tetrazona* and *B. pentazona*) are also quite prolific breeders. The two forms can be distinguished by the number of vertical stripes across their bodies. They are similar to Rosy Barbs in their requirements, but cannot be trusted in a community tank with long-finned fish, because they are bad 'nippers'. Individuals often prove worse in this respect than a school, possibly because they lack the distinct pecking order which evolves therein. The Five-banded form (*B. pentazona*) is the more reliable community member.

One of the smaller species, rarely exceeding 6 cm (2.5 in), is the Black Ruby Barb, which is a native of Sri Lanka. They prefer a slightly higher temperature than other barbs, about 26°C (79°F) suiting them well. Males develop a rich red tinge to the lower part of their bodies when in breeding condition. In contrast, the Tinfoil Barb (*B. schwanenfeldi*) may attain a length of 30 cm (12 in) or more. It is a striking fish, with a bright metallic silver body and reddish markings on its fins. They require a correspondingly large set-up, taking into account their size, and are best kept in groups. Tinfoil Barbs have healthy appetites, and bigger specimens will take meat such as ox heart and dog food, which must be soaked thoroughly beforehand if necessary. The water in their aquarium needs to be kept clean and well-aerated. They are rather susceptible to chlorine or excessive amounts of carbon dioxide dissolved in the water.

Tiger Barb (*Barbus tetrazona*).

An unusual African barb is *B. callensis*, known also as the Moroccan Barb. This inhabits hot water springs, and is reputed to be able to survive in very high temperatures. Apart from Morocco, it occurs in parts of Algeria and Spain. Because it requires an average temperature of 30°C (86°F), this barb will probably need a tank to itself. The attractive yellowish Congo Barb (*B. callipterus*) is not as free-breeding as its Asian relatives. Further south, the Banded Barb (*B. fasciolatus*) occurs in Angola and likewise is rarely seen in aquaria. This species is bluish-green in colour.

Danios Two members of the genus *Danio* are well-known to aquarists. The Bengal Danio (*D. devario*) from India reaches a size of about 10 cm (4 in) and is silvery-green in colour. It is less often seen than the Giant Danio (*D. aequipinnatus*), found naturally in western parts of India as well as Sri Lanka. The predominant colour in this fish is steely-blue, with yellowish bands running along the body. Females are usually bigger than males, reaching 15 cm (6 in), and their central blue stripe is said to curl more near the tail. This species should be kept in schools with fish of similar size, because they may occasionally eat smaller individuals.

Danios will adapt to quite a wide temperature range, between 21° and 27°C (70°-80°F), and are undemanding with regard to pH and hardness of the water, providing it is not extreme. They take flaked foods readily, and livefood is a very useful conditioner. When breeding, danios should be provided with a tank containing fine-leaved vegetation. A temperature of 26°-27°C (78°-80°F) will induce spawning, and the female should be allowed to settle in the tank for a day before two males are introduced. The adults must all

Zebra Danios (*Brachydanio rerio*).

then be removed before they can eat the eggs, which should hatch in a day. The female may well be ready to breed again about a month later.

Other danios belonging to the genus *Brachydanio* are often kept. The Pearl or Gold Danio (*B. albolineatus*) is a fairly ready breeder, which typically spawns in the morning, being stimulated by sunlight. This species may produce over 200 eggs, but the fish will rapidly consume them if they are given the opportunity. Zebra Danios (*B. rerio*), so-named because of the striped pattern of their markings, are amongst the easiest species to spawn successfully. They can be kept safely in schools with other small fish. Females can be recognized by their rounded bellies. A slightly small species, about 3.75 cm (1½ in) in length, is the Spotted Danio (*B. nigrofasciatus*). This fish is often more reluctant to breed than the previous danios, although the fry are not hard to rear on infusoria and then brine shrimps.

Spotted Danios (*Brachydanio nigrofasciatus*).

Rasboras Rasboras are confined to south-east Asia, where approximately thirty species are found. They are shoaling fish, and out of the dozen species which are often available, although they adapt well to aquarium conditions, breeding successes are rare. This may be because they are communal breeders, or it may be a reflection on the composition of their water. It is known that they require acid water, with a relatively high concentration of iron, and naturally spawn in masses of cryptocornes and other similar broad-leaved plants. Their eggs are laid on the under-surface of the leaves.

Rasboras nevertheless make attractive aquarium occupants, and can be quite long-lived. They require a temperature similar to danios, and are peaceful in a community tank. Sexing is very difficult in most species, although there are exceptions, as in the case of the Brilliant Rasbora (*Rasbora einthoveni*), the male of which has a purple tinge. The Harlequin Fish or Red Rasbora (*R. heteromorpha*) is one of the most attractive members of the group, and like Hengel's Rasbora (*R. hengeli*) it requires soft, acid water

Right Red Rasbora (*Rasbora heteromorpha*).

Below Scissortail Rasbora (*Rasbora trilineata*).

(pH 5.6-6.4; DH less than 8). When kept under different conditions, it is said to become sterile. Both these species reach less than 5 cm (2 in) in length.

Scissortail Rasboras (*R. trilineata*) are characterized by their distinctive tails. Like other related species, they are omnivorous, but prefer livefoods. The Scissortail is a relatively hardy rasbora, and does not require such shaded conditions as the preceding species. It can grow to 15 cm (6 in), but rarely attains this size under aquarium conditions. The Yellow Rasbora (*R. elegans*), which is rather greyer than its name suggests, is another larger species. It can grow to 13 cm (5 in) and mature females lack the brown tinge seen in the anal fins of males.

For those attempting to breed rasboras, gnat larvae are a good conditioner. The female will spawn in a water temperature of 27°C (80°F) on suitable plants, and is often stimulated by rays of sunlight. In some cases, such as the Red Rasbora, although the eggs are often unmolested, the fry, which hatch about a day later, may well be eaten by the adults. Once free-swimming, the young fish will require infusoria or a suitable substitute. The Eye-spot Rasbora (*R. dorsiocellata*), named after the black spot on its dorsal fin, is one of the easiest species to breed successfully.

Other miscellaneous cyprinids

The Flying Fox (*Epalzeorhynchus kalopterus*) and its relative (*E. siamensis*), which was discovered during the 1950s, are useful members of a community tank. They require relatively soft water and a temperature of 23°-27°C (74°-80°F), and being found naturally in fast-flowing water, are correspondingly active. *E. siamensis* is a larger species, with a more yellowish body.

The mouths of these fish are adapted to graze on algae, and also

Flying Fox (*Epalzeorhynchus kalopterus*).

Red-tailed shark (*Labeo bicolor*).

serve to anchor them in a particular locality, against a strong current. They live around the bottom of a tank, where they should be provided with suitable hiding places. Apart from consuming algae, Flying Foxes will also eat any *Planaria* which inadvertently are allowed access to the tank, as well as boiled spinach and various proprietary foods. There appears to be no information concerning their breeding habits.

Another cyprinid fish, in spite of its misleading name, which feeds on algae is the Red-tailed Shark (*Labeo bicolor*). It does best in a well-planted aquarium, with soft, acid water maintained at a temperature of 24°-26°C (75°-79°F). Natives of Thailand, these fish tend to become rather quarrelsome amongst themselves as they get bigger. They are very agile swimmers, and difficult to catch as a result. The bright red coloration of their tails can be improved by colour feeding, and although omnivorous, Red-tailed Black Sharks must have some vegetable matter, such as algae, cooked oatmeal or boiled spinach available.

Breeding details of this species do not appear to have been recorded, but the closely related Red-fin Shark (*L. frenatus*) has been spawned successfully in an aquarium. They appear to mature at about 7.5 cm (3 in) in length and are often very aggressive at spawning time. Males alone care for the eggs until they hatch, which in a temperature of 24°C (75°F) will take about two days. The fry, which may emerge without yolk sacs, can be reared on infusoria and then brine shrimps and spinach. The adults in one case were left safely with the fry after hatching, taking them to shelter if there appeared to be any risk of danger. By the age of seven weeks, there were about 150 fry from this spawning and these had grown to about 1.87 cm (¾ in) in length. A duller member of this genus which is sometimes available is the Harlequin Shark (*L. variegatus*), which hails from Upper Zaire in Africa. Its requirements are similar to those of the preceding species.

Tetras and related species

Members of the family Characidae have a wide distribution through Africa and tropical America. They are characterized predominantly by the presence of teeth and the development of an adipose fin. Over 100 species have been kept successfully in aquaria, and the family includes some of the most colourful freshwater species. They are not difficult fish to cater for, requiring a water temperature between 21° and 24°C (70°-75°F). Although some are mainly vegetarian in their feeding habits and others carnivorous, they will live well together if given a mixed diet supplemented with livefood. Unfortunately they are not frequently bred in aquaria, but some successes have been achieved by providing soft water heated to 28°C (82°F), with plenty of vegetation in the tank where females can scatter their adhesive eggs. These will be eaten, however, if the adult fish are not removed after laying has occurred.

Distribution of the characins.

The colourful tetras are a particular favourite of many aquarists. The Neon (*Hyphessobrycon innesi*) and Cardinal (*Cheirodon axelrodi*) are among the most commonly available species. When the Neon Tetra was first introduced to aquarists in 1936 however, it commanded a price of $40, which was equivalent in real terms to an average month's salary at that time. Coming from the headwaters of the Amazon, these fish should be kept in schools along with other peaceable fish of similar size, such as small rasboras, barbs or even other tetras. They require relatively dark surroundings, and clean, well-aerated soft water, with a pH tending towards an acid reading (6.0-6.5). This is a carnivorous species, and should be fed accordingly using prepared foods as well as livefood. They often prefer to eat food which is slowly sinking in the tank. Neon Tetras are regarded as being slightly delicate by some aquarists, especially when young. They are susceptible to Neon Tetra disease, which results in a loss of pigmentation, and is caused by a *Microspordium* parasite, called *Plistophora hyphessobryconis*.

Spawning tanks for these tetras must have dark bottoms, and be kept shaded, as their eggs are sensitive to excessive light. Egg-laying may take three hours or so, during which time perhaps 150 eggs will have been produced. The parents must then be removed. The eggs should hatch in about a day, and the fry will be swimming freely four days later. The youngsters should be kept in the same tank water if possible for the first two months of life, because they can react badly to being moved to fresh water. The Black form of the Neon Tetra (*Hyphessobrycon herbertaxelrodi*) occurs in parts of Brazil, and has similar needs. Other tetras of this genus include the Blood Characin (*H. callistus*) and the Bleeding Heart Tetra (*H. ornatus*). Neither is easy to sex.

An unusual species is the Blind Cave Characin (*Astyanax jordani*), which is found in the subterranean caves of the Rio

Cardinal Tetras *(Cheirodon axelrodi)*.

Neon Tetras (*Hyphessobrycon innesi*).

Bleeding Heart Tetra (*Hyphessobrycon ornatus*).

Panuco in Mexico. They are not difficult to maintain in aquaria, and an artificial cave structure can be easily constructed using rockwork and slate. The sensory lateral line is well-developed in these fish. Another tetra with a slightly bizarre appearance is the X-ray Fish (*Pristella riddlei*) which is semi-transparent. Males in this case are more colourful than females. They can lay up to 300 eggs during a single spawning, but these will be eaten unless the adults are separated from them.

Right Blood Characin (*Hyphessobrycon callistus*).

Above X-ray Fish (*Pristella riddlei*).

Tetras belonging to the genus *Moenkhausia* are similar to previous species in their requirements, requiring water with a DH of about 10°, and an acid pH which can be achieved by filtering through peat. They have more conspicuous scales than other tetras, and, being omnivorous, may nibble at plants growing in their tank. *Ephippicharax orbicularis* needs a similar tank set-up, with an area for swimming at the front and some tough plants like *Echinodorus* around the perimeter. Floating vegetation on the surface provides both shade and a ready source of food.

Ephippicharax orbicularis.

Piranha (*Pygocentrus piraya*). This species can grow to 60 cm (2 ft) in length.

The most notorious characins are undoubtedly the piranhas, of which four species are recognized. These fish occur naturally in shoals, but in aquarium surroundings smaller individuals may be cannibalized by their fellows and they are best kept singly. Piranhas are, in fact, relatively sluggish fish, and apart from their supposed novelty value, do not make very attractive tank occupants. They require soft, slightly acid water and restricted lighting. Young piranhas can be fed on tubifex and whiteworm, while larger fish will consume ox heart and earthworms. The keeping of piranhas is banned in certain areas, such as the state of Florida, because of fears over deliberate irresponsible releases of these fish, and the resulting potential damage to native fish stocks, as has been seen in Australia.

African characins are less streamlined than their American relatives, but require similar conditions, with adequate space for swimming. They range in size from the Long-finned Characin (*Alestes longipinnis*) which can reach 14 cm (5½ in) down to the Congo Tetra (*Micralestes interruptus*) which is only about 7.5 cm (3 in) in length.

Cichlids

Members of the family Cichlidae have a very wide distribution, and while some, such as the angelfish, are well-known to aquarists, others occurring in the Rift Valley Lakes are often rarities which command high prices. Cichlids, with some exceptions, are not good inmates for the community tank, and should really form part of a more specialized collection. They tend to be bullies, and are often destructive.

The two species of Asian cichlid are quite scarce, although the Orange Chromide (*Eltroplus maculatus*) may be seen occasionally. This species is not aggressive or destructive, but is rather sensitive to water changes. Amongst the South American forms, one of the

Distribution of cichlids.

Ramirez's Dwarf Cichlid (*Apistogramma ramirezi*).

most desirable is the Blue Acara (*Hequidens pulcher*), which is omnivorous and relatively peaceful, growing to a length of only 15 cm (6 in). Eggs are usually laid on suitable rockwork rather than vegetation, and both parents then look after the young fry.

Dwarf cichlids require a similar water temperature, about 24°C (75°F), and a maximum hardness of 10°DH along with an acid pH. These fish are more delicate than their larger relatives, and must have adequate shelter in their tanks, as well as swimming space. Males are generally bigger and more colourful. Spawn is deposited in a prepared cavity, and in the case of *Apistogramma ramirezi*, both adults care for their offspring. The eggs hatch in about four days, and brine shrimps can be used as a rearing food along with chopped whiteworm.

One of the most spectacular cichlids is undoubtedly the Oscar, also known as the Velvet Cichlid (*Astronotus ocellatus*), which can attain a length of nearly 35 cm (14 in). Even if small when acquired, these fish will ultimately need a large tank to themselves. They are not easily bred, but lay on rockwork which they clean beforehand. The brood may number as many as 1000 fry, which are concentrated protectively in an area by their parents, but only about 300 are likely to survive under good conditions. Fry will often consume each other, and they have large appetites. A red form of the Oscar is now being bred in increasing numbers.

There are various other smaller but aggressive South American cichlids often available. These include the Jack Dempsey (*Cichlasoma octofasciatum*), named after the famous boxer, and the smaller

Oscar (*Astronotus ocellatus*).

Opposite page, top *Pterophyllum scalare*, normal form.

Opposite page, bottom *Pterophyllum scalare*, a selected mottled form.

Zebra or Convict Cichlid (*C. nigrofasciatum*) which grows to nearly 10 cm (4 in). A water temperature of 21°C (72°F) suits these fish well. Both have a tendency to dig into the aquarium substrate, and will uproot plants in the process.

Angelfish are amongst the most popular aquarium fish, possessing a very elegant shape and motion. Youngsters are often sold for community tanks, but angelfish should be kept alone in individual

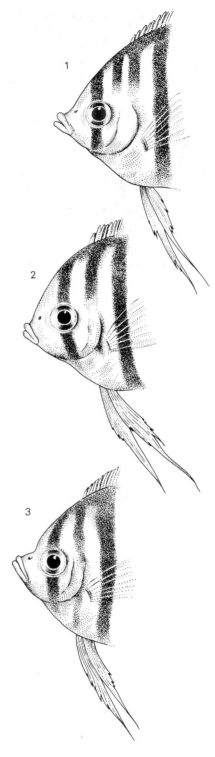

The three species of *Pterophyllum* can be distinguished by the shape of the head:
1 *P. dumerilii;*
2 *P. scalare;*
3 *P. altum.*

Right Discus (*Symphysodon aequifasciata*). This species occurs from the mouth of the Amazon to Peru.

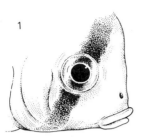

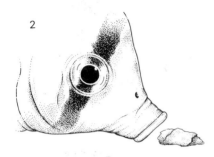

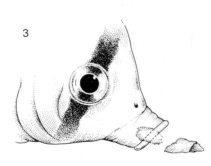

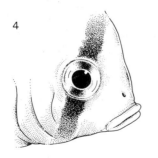

Method of feeding in *Pterophyllum*:
1 the food is seen;
2 the mouth is protruded;
3 the food is sucked in;
4 the mouth returns to its original position.

shoals for several reasons. They have a fast rate of growth, and will often outpace other members of the tank, while their elaborate fins invite nipping. Angelfish are predominantly carnivorous in their feeding habits, and will readily consume the eggs and fry of other fish sharing their accommodation. By virtue of their shape, and the fact that they can grow to 15 cm (6 in), these cichlids require a fairly deep tank, planted with suitable vegetation such as *Vallisneria gigantea*.

Their water should be at a temperature of 24°C (75°F) raised a couple of degrees for spawning purposes. A slightly acid pH, about 6.8, is preferable. They will often spawn on slate, and guard the eggs and resulting fry. Various mutations of the angelfish are now established, with such exotic names as 'Butterballs'. These fish become bright yellow as they mature, and were developed initially over a four-year period by Carl Naja in America.

Another very attractive South American cichlid, which requires rather special management, is the Discus, of which two species are recognized. *Symphysodon* requires very soft water, with a DH reading in the range 1-5, and an acid pH of 6.2-6.6. They are very susceptible to infection by the protozoan *Hexamita*, and various gill-flukes, and cannot be recommended for the novice aquarist. Several attractive colour variants of the discus have been bred successfully, including a turquoise form produced by Jack Wattley in Florida.

Apart from the specialist African Rift Lake cichlids, other species occur in lakes and rivers elsewhere on the continent. Members of the genus *Tilapia* have even been introduced successfully in other countries, ranging across South-east Asia to Hawaii. These

Left Turquoise form of the Discus.

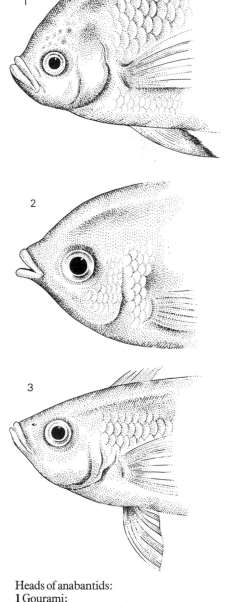

fish are known as mouth-brooders, and some, such as the Mozambique species (*T. mossambica*), can grow quite large, over 30 cm (12 in).

Labyrinth fish

Members of the family Anabantidae have a unique anatomical adaptation, referred to as the labyrinth organ, which allows them to breathe air at the water's surface. They usually live in areas of muddy water with a low oxygen content, and must take in atmospheric oxygen in order to survive. The Paradise Fish (*Macropodus opercularis*) found in eastern parts of Asia is a typical member of this group. They are often rather too aggressive for the community tank, and should really be kept on their own. Water which is medium-hard and heated to 24°C (75°F) will meet their needs, while the tank itself should be densely planted, complete with floating vegetation.

Glass jars containing the brightly-coloured Fighting Fish (*Betta splendens*) never fail to attract attention in aquarist shops, and various mutant forms are also available. Males, as their name suggests, will fight ferociously among themselves, and, with their long flowing fins, are best kept out of a community tank. A small aquarium, only 60 cm (24 in) in length, and a temperature slightly higher than for the preceding species, will suit them well. Females

Heads of anabantids:
1 Gourami;
2 Kissing Gourami;
3 Climbing Perch.

Haplochromis moorii. A mouth-brooding cichlid found in Lake Malawi. Both sexes of this species develop a prominent forehead.

Fighting Fish (*Betta splendens*). Three males of different colour forms.

Fighting Fish
mating.

are much less conspicuous than males, with smaller fins. At breeding time, the male entwines with his mate and is responsible for transferring the eggs to the bubble nest, characteristic of these and other anabantids. The fry emerge in about two days, and, after consuming their egg sacs, will take infusoria.

The gouramis also belong to this family, and are much more suitable for the community tank, although problems may arise at spawning time. The Kissing Gourami (*Helostoma temmincki*), from south-east Asia, has developed elaborate lips for feeding on algae, and 'kissing' contacts can occasionally be observed between two individuals. *Trichogaster* species such as the Pearl Gourami (*T. leeri*) are also popular aquarium fish, requiring medium-hard water with a temperature of 26°C (79°F), and a mixed diet. The Chocolate Gourami (*Sphaerichthys osphromenoides*) is an exception from other gouramis, as it must be kept in very soft water, with an acid pH (0-3°DH; pH 6 or less), which is heated to 28°C (82°F). It is not recommended as an introduction to the group, being more delicate than other species. Although African anabantids, belonging to the genus *Ctenopoma* are sometimes available, they are not suitable for the mixed tank, proving aggressive and carnivorous.

Pearl Gourami *(Trichogaster leeri)*.

Spotted Climbing Perch *(Ctenopoma acutirostre)* from Zaire. An aggressive fish, which can reach 15 cm (6 in) in length.

Pearl Gouramis will breed in the typical manner of the family, often choosing to build a nest amongst Indian Fern. Males of this species rarely get aggressive towards females after spawning. The eggs hatch in two days, and may yield up to 1000 fry. The spawning tank, as for all labyrinths, must be covered, to prevent excessive losses when the young start breathing atmospheric air which is potentially too cold. Overcrowding will also reduce their numbers dramatically, so the tank should have a large surface area. These can be prolific fish however, and over eighteen months, it is possible to rear as many as 5000 fry successfully from a pair. They require infusoria at first, and finely-sieved egg yolk, followed by brine shrimps.

Catfish

The catfish are a very large group, with over 2000 recognized species divided into twenty families. Many are, however, unsuitable for the community aquarium because they grow too large, and this aspect should be considered before purchasing a particular species. Catfish possess characteristic sensory barbels close to their mouths, which may have a feathery or unbranched structure. Many are semi-nocturnal, preferring to scavenge for food during the hours of darkness.

The armoured *Corydoras* catfish are a favourite group for the aquarium, partly because of their relatively small size. They rarely exceed 10 cm (4 in), and are quite active during daylight. These catfish are suitable for a community tank, where they will consume food left by other inhabitants. Several should be kept together if possible, under soft water conditions with a neutral pH reading. *Corydoras* Catfish will breed in the aquarium. Females become swollen with eggs prior to spawning, and should be placed with several males in a lightly planted tank lined with sand, in a temperature of 26°C (79°F). Once a pair is formed, the other males should be removed, and after spawning, these fish must be returned to the community tank because they will eat their eggs. These are laid in batches, numbering a maximum of 300 eggs in total. They should hatch in about a week, and the fry must be offered infusoria at first.

The Bronze Corydoras (*C. aeneus*) is one of the easiest species to breed successfully. Their tank should contain adequate hiding places, as with all catfish. Spawning typically occurs from about October onwards, being stimulated by livefoods, such as tubifex. They will gulp air directly from the surface, which is a natural adaptation for survival in poorly-oxygenated waters. The two

Bronze Corydoras (*Corydoras aeneus*).

Upside-down Catfish (*Synodontis nigriventris*).

smallest members of the genus are less commonly seen. The Pygmy Catfish (*C. nastatus*) reaches a size of about 4 cm (1½ in)¦, whereas *C. cochui* is approximately 1.25 cm (½ in) shorter.

Amongst other catfish, those belonging to the family Mochocidae are essentially nocturnal. The unusual Upside-down Catfish (*Synodontis nigriventris*) belongs to this group. It swims upside-down, and thus can feed on the under-surface of leaves. Its pattern of camouflage is also reversed. Two more colourful members of this African genus are *S. angelicus* and *S. flavitaeniatus*, although these tend to lose their markings as they get older.

Synodontis angelicus **above**, with *Synodontis flavitaeniatus* **below**. The markings of these fish tend to fade as they grow older.

Spiny eels and loaches

Spiny eels, like many catfish, are essentially nocturnal. They often occur in brackish water, so salt should be added to their aquarium water. *Macrognathus aculeatus* can reach a size of 35 cm (13¾ in) whereas another Asian form, *Mastacembelus armatus* may grow as large as 80 cm (31 in). Spiny eels feed largely on worms of various types, and should be kept in a tank with a sandy bottom, into which they will burrow, leaving only their heads exposed. They tend to be aggressive, and are rather specialized in their needs.

Acanthophthalmus loaches may at first sight appear similar to spiny eels, by virtue of their long thin bodies. They require similar conditions, and are also more active under conditions of subdued lighting. The various species of this genus are known as Coolie Loaches, and reach a size of about 8 cm (3 in). They have a spike in front of their eyes that can inflict a painful stab to catch the unwary, and will take air directly from the water's surface. These loaches

Above Spiny Eel (*Mastacembelus armatus*).

Right An *Acanthophthalmus* loach.

need soft water, with a DH not in excess of 10°, and a temperature between 24° and 28°C (75°-82°F). They will take a varied diet, and scavenge effectively in the tank. Breeding in artificial conditions is uncommon.

Various other loaches are sometimes available, including the rather aggressive Tiger Loach (*Botia hymenophysa*). The colourful Mouse Botia (*B. horae*) is, by way of contrast, fairly peaceful and requires a temperature of not more than 26°C (79°F). Clown

Loaches (*B. macracantha*) are equally attractive, and need soft water conditions.

Another useful loach for the community tank is *Gyrinocheilus aymonieri*, which will consume algae. These fish like well-oxygenated, clean water and a temperature in the range of 20°-28°C (68°-82°F). They have a sucker mouth, and can adhere to rockwork or even the sides of a tank. Since they are then unable to take in water, they have evolved an extra orifice to enable water to continue flowing over each set of gills. Sucker loaches should not be kept alongside elongated fish, because they may attach themselves accordingly, and damage the skin of their hosts.

Left Tiger Loach *(Botia hymenophysa)*.

Below Mouse Botia *(Botia horae)*.

Gyrinocheilus aymonieri

Hatchetfish

Members of this group are not always easy fish to maintain successfully, and are rarely bred in aquaria. Hatchetfish, with their unusual shape, live near the water's surface, and are reported to be able to fly above it as well, using their pectoral fins. They must be kept in a covered tank, and be fed livefoods such as fruitflies sprinkled on the surface. Hatchetfish are not really suitable for the newcomer to the hobby of fish-keeping.

Marbled Hatchetfish (*Carnegiella strigata*).

Pencilfish

These fish are placed in the family Hemiodontidae, only possessing teeth in the upper jaw, although they are otherwise rather similar to characins, in spite of their slender, elongated shape. They require a well-planted tank with adequate cover, where they will often stay relatively motionless unless threatened. Soft water conditions, with a temperature of 24°-26°C (75°-79°F) and livefood will keep them in good health. The Three-banded Pencilfish (*Nannostomus tri-fasciatus*) and related members of this genus are unique because their markings alter between day and night time. They are rarely bred, and invariably prove bad egg-eaters if given the opportunity.

Three-banded Pencilfish (*Nannostomus trifasciatus*).

Headstanders

These are unusual fish, which often prove difficult to acclimatize to new surroundings successfully. Headstanders remain vertical in the water for long periods, concealing themselves amongst suitable vegetation. They are best kept in shoals in fairly large well-planted tanks that should always be covered. These fish are adept at feeding on algae, and will also consume various worms and other livefood.

Elephant-nosed fish

A playful species with an unusual appearance is the Elephant-nosed Fish (*Gnathonemus petersi*), a member of the Mormyrid family. The mouth in this fish has evolved to form a proboscis. They need a temperature of about 24°C (75°F) and adequate hiding areas in the tank, as can be provided by roots and rocks. Dim lighting suits them best, and the water should be soft. They need plenty of livefood and may grow to a maximum size of nearly 20 cm (8 in). If two young specimens are kept together, they will often play with a small ball made of tinfoil floating on the water in their aquarium. Larger groups should not be housed in the same tank,

Head of a mormyrid.

Striped Anostomus (*Anostomus anostomus*) – one of the most attractive of the headstanders.

because they produce electrical currents which can disorientate others nearby. This characteristic serves as an additional sensory device, and in conjunction with it, mormyrids have evolved a correspondingly large brain. They do not appear to have been bred successfully in aquaria as yet, and older individuals may quarrel amongst themselves.

Elephant-nosed Fish (*Gnathonemus petersi*).

An aquarium for these fish should include a muddy or sandy area on the base if possible, rather than having a floor covering comprised entirely of gravel. This will then enable the fish to probe here in search of small worms and other creatures.

Although aggressive towards their own kind, it is quite possible to include a single Elephant-nosed fish in a community aquarium, in the company of other non-aggressive species such as Congo Tetras (*Micralestes interruptus*). While Elephant-nosed Fish show a distinct preference for livefood, they can be persuaded to eat dried foods.

Bibliography

The following titles may be useful for further reading:

Cole, Peter *The Art of Goldfish Keeping* Blandford, 1995
Cole, Peter *The Art of Koi Keeping* Blandford, 1990 and 1993.
Dawes, John *Livebearing Fishes* Blandford, 1991 and 1995
Lambert, Derek & Pat *Platies and Swordtails* 'An Aquarist's Handbook' Blandford, 1995
Lambourne, Derek *Corydoras Catfish* 'An Aquarist's Handbook' Blandford 1995
Mojetta, Angelo *The Aquarium – A Complete Guide* Blandford 1993

There are, in addition, various periodicals which are likely to be of interest. These include:

The Aquarist & Pondkeeper
Practical Fishkeeping
Tropical Fish Hobbyist (USA)

Index

Page numbers in *italics* refer to illustrations.